MONEY
How to Get It,
Keep It,
and Make It Grow

MONEY
How to Get It, Keep It, and Make It Grow

Michael Hayes

amacom

A Division of American Management Associations

TO the memory of my father,
Robert Eugene Hayes,
who taught me the value of a dollar
(when a dollar had value).

Library of Congress Cataloging in Publication Data

Hayes, Michael, 1939–
    Money: how to get it, keep it, and make it grow.

    Includes index.
    1. Finance, Personal. 2. Success. 3. Investments.
I. Title.
HG179.H35   332'.024   78-27414
ISBN 0-8144-5503-4

© 1979 AMACOM
A division of American Management Associations, New
York.
All rights reserved. Printed in the United States of
America.

First Printing

Acknowledgments

FEW works of any substance are the effort of a single person, so I'd like to express my appreciation to my old-time buddies Jim Kelly and Connie Shelnut, who gave me their good ideas and threw out a few of my bad ones; to Catherine Osen and Jack Syfrig, who transformed my rambling pontifications into readable English; and especially to Jennifer Zehner, who labored over several manuscript drafts and served as my mental partner. Jack Syfrig also did the graphics, an exacting task, well done.

Don Harless, one of the best students I've had in my days as a professor, and his lovely wife, Jan, deserve my deepest thanks. Don and Jan are the very people for whom this book is written: young, smart, and concerned about the future while fully enjoying the present. They spent many hours of their valuable time on this effort and I'm grateful for both their assistance and their friendship.

The support and encouragement of Karen Georgatos made my life a whole lot happier.

Preface

MOTHER NATURE has the rather distasteful habit of shattering most of our grandiose schemes, particularly the kind that involve almost no effort and a promise to get us rich. She has, in fact, screwed up our designs so often and so consistently that her untimely interferences have been formally codified into Murphy's Law: *If anything can go wrong, it will.* What have Mother Nature and Murphy's Law got to do with a book about money? Everything. If it weren't for Mother and Murphy, getting rich would be much simpler than it is. But apparently their job is to make sure that the rich remain a small minority, so they've got to make suckers out of anyone who thinks it's easy to get rich quick.

At times it does look easy—maybe even too easy. But yesterday's "sure thing" all too often turns into a total disaster for the unwary. Just ask the guy who borrowed money to buy stocks ten years ago, when they were in their heyday, and watched quotes fall by two-thirds in the next six years; or the guy who bought gold the day it became legal, only to watch bullion prices drop in half during the next eighteen months.

Yes, Mother and Murphy are always working to crush something just when it looks like it absolutely cannot lose, and they
make certain that there ain't no easy way for you to get rich.

O.K., scratch the easy route. Is there *any* way? Yes—and on
just a few bucks a day! You can get there if you *plan to be rich,*
if you *pay yourself first* every month, and if you *manage your
money* wisely. I estimate that, starting from ground zero, $3 a
day should be worth not less than $20,000 in ten years, and
maybe $200,000 or so thirty years from now. That's one hell
of a claim, but if the next fifty years are anything like the last,
you'll be able to do it.

The most telling part of any book is its conclusion. It lets
you know whether the writer had anything to say or not. In
this book the conclusion is short, so you can read it while
you're standing at the stacks. Go ahead. It will tell you why I
wrote it in the first place and why I think you can learn from
my mistakes. If you decide to take it home, I hope that you'll
find reading it from cover to cover a profitable experience.

Michael Hayes

Contents

If You Want It,
If You Need It,
You Can Get It

THINK you can run $3 a day into a minor fortune—say, $20,000 or more in ten years, or upwards of $100,000 in twenty years? That's the plot, so let's sit down and talk about money for a while.

On the theory that you shouldn't have to plunk down the price of this book just to find out the general theme, I'm going to tell you right at the start what the next two hundred pages have to say. To begin with, I'm serious when I say that you can build a fortune on your own. One minor qualifier: other than sheer luck, there's no practical way to get rich overnight; you'll never accumulate much wealth unless you're willing to work at it. But if you resolve to combine some study and effort with a measure of discipline, and if you then use a common-sense method for recognizing opportunity and avoiding disaster, you can make it happen. Money—how to get it, keep it, and make it grow—is what I want to talk to you about.

If you're ready to stop being conned by a "buy now, pay later" system designed to keep you perpetually broke, if you're willing to learn how to plan your way to wealth, and if you can devote some energy to the investment process, then virtually nothing stands between you and wealth. Once we've examined the methods, I think you'll agree that there are steady, proven, and conservative techniques that can help you climb into a higher financial bracket. This book won't help you pick the winning lottery ticket, but it will provide you with the background information and the specific approach you'll need to build financial security in a systematic, unspectacular manner. And you'll be able to do it on your own. So let's look at *you*.

You're likely to earn over half a million dollars by working your tail off in the next thirty or forty years. How would you like to have something to show for all that effort? The simple fact is that every one of us needs money, and most of us know a few people who already have ingenious schemes for raising a fortune. But chances are that the riches they lust after will never be theirs. The sad reality is that although practically any working person, and that includes you and me, can become rich, most people have absolutely no idea how to go about acquiring wealth, or, having acquired it, how to make it work for them. First and foremost, getting rich requires a master plan. For lack of that plan, most people will exit this life as unendowed as when they entered it. The overwhelming majority will never know the financial freedom that could have been theirs had they been able to hang onto a few bucks a day.

I promise you that if you have a decent job, there's a real alternative to just scraping by. That alternative is to do some planning, to *think your way to wealth*. The process of getting money, keeping it, and making it work for you requires, more than anything else, a plan for systematically *setting aside a few dollars every day*. Do that for the next few years and you'll have a substantial amount ten or twenty years from now.

Money is one of the strongest motivators in any economic society. And like those other primary activators, love and power, money is poorly understood. Love is more than sex, power is more than authority, and money is more than just a medium of exchange. Money is *security* in the sense that you don't have to worry about the next payment. Money is *independence* in the sense that you don't have to tolerate an undeserved hassle from anyone. Of course, some people chase money as a source of power; to them, it represents the power to command instead of being commanded. And reflecting our somewhat twisted societal values, money begets status. It's the visible yardstick too many of us use to measure who is on top. These are the hidden appeals of money—security, independence, power, and status. Where status and power are concerned, it can't be denied that money talks. The sound of a buck can be heard anywhere. The common thread in the need for money, however, is that it enhances our freedom to choose our own way . . . to decide for ourselves what we will do and be.

My own aspirations for security and independence make it absolutely essential to know how to get money, how to keep it, and how to make it work for me. You feel that way too? Or do I hear you saying, "Now wait a minute. Why are you going on about this financial freedom fantasy when I'm more worried about keeping the credit cards up to date?" All right, I'll agree that it's senseless to talk about a million dollars when neither of us would have an easy time recognizing a megabuck.

So let's change perspectives. Let's concentrate on a time frame and a dollar amount we can both understand. Let's concentrate on the hard part—designing a plan for getting the first twenty thousand in the next few years. Once we've developed the plan, the follow-through is up to you. And once you've built the first twenty grand, you'll be able to envision the next fifty pretty easily. It's like the first step you took as a kid—it gave you the confidence to take the next, and before you knew it, you were off and running. It's the same with money. The knowledge that you can do it, based on your past successes, will carry you through to financial freedom. So let's concentrate on those first few steps.

Probably the strongest and most pressing reason for accumulating money today is the need to assure financial freedom at the end of our working years. Each of us eventually faces retirement. Whether it comes at forty-five or at sixty-five, it's followed by a period that can be either a reward or a penalty; the choice is ours. If you're financially prepared for the drastic reduction in earning capability, retirement can be filled with opportunities to enjoy the benefits of your long years of labor. But your capacity to enjoy life at retirement will be severely restricted if all you have are the meager provisions of Social Security or a small pension. In that event, the years that should have been a payoff will be merely a continuation of the battle to survive. The difference between fulfillment and bare survival is the money you've managed to accumulate. That choice needs to be made early. By the time you're fifty, it will be too late to get started.

Very few working men and women are able to face the prospect of retirement with high expectations. In fact, only about one person in fifty leaves this world with an estate of $200,000 or more. It may sound huge, but $200,000 is not a large amount of money in proportion to what you can reasonably expect to earn over the years, and it's a very reasonable goal to set for yourself if you have twenty-five more working years left. Of course, if you have thirty or forty years remaining, it won't take much sacrifice at all to accumulate $200,000; you may even decide to become richer. But you won't be able to do it unless you're willing to give up a few dollars every single day of your working life. You've got a few bucks coming in every day, and more than a few years left, so $200,000 should be no problem once you decide to *pay yourself first*.

How Much? How Fast?

"O.K.," you say. "You've got my attention. But I've got a perfectly logical question as this point. If it's so damn easy to get that way, why isn't everyone rich? Obviously there are a lot of people who make decent money, but most of them never get rich. There must be some reason."

Right. There are several reasons. But the primary reason the not-rich outnumber the rich so heavily is that most people don't know how to *make their money make money*.

The most critical of the factors over which you have any degree of control is the rate at which your investment capital grows—in other words, how hard your money works for you. You don't have much control over the period of time your plan is to run, since you've got a fixed number of years left before you retire. You have some control over the amount of your monthly payments to yourself, but that choice is narrowly restricted by your present level of income and your other obligations—for living, entertainment, and so on. But you do have effective control over the earning rate, the rate of return, on your investments. And if you are really serious about acquiring money, you can't afford to settle for low rates of return.

By selecting only those investments that offer higher rates of return, and by applying management techniques that have proven themselves in the past, you can expect your money to compound faster. As it does, your monthly paycheck to your future will create more and more wealth for you. Table 1-1 gives you an example. If you were to invest only $50 each month for ten years, and if you earned only 6% per year compounded, you would accumulate a final total of $7900 on a total investment of $6000; after twenty-five years you would have about $32,900 on a $15,000 investment. At that rate, all those years of scrimping and saving would hardly have been

Table 1-1. Wealth accumulated on an investment of $50 a month (figures rounded to nearest $100).

Amount Invested	Years	Rate of Return			
		6%	*10%*	*14%*	*18%*
$ 3,000	5	$ 3,400	$ 3,700	$ 4,000	$ 4,300
6,000	10	7,900	9,600	11,600	14,100
9,000	15	14,000	19,100	26,300	36,600
12,000	20	22,100	34,400	54,600	88,000
15,000	25	32,900	59,000	109,100	205,600
30,000	30	47,400	98,700	214,100	474,600

worth the effort. On the other hand, if you managed to earn 18% instead of 6%, the same $50 every month would be worth $14,100 after ten years and a whopping $205,600 after twenty-five years. Of course, if you were able to sock away $100 a month, you'd end up with twice that amount. And *that's* something to get excited about!

At miserly earning rates like those paid by banks and insurance companies, your investment dollars simply don't work as hard as they can for you. Yeah, there are some short-term risks associated with most of the high-return media, but you can't get a guarantee and a high return in the same investment. After all, if the banks and insurance companies can afford to maintain their headquarters in those prestigious buildings, and if they can cover all of their operating costs, turn a healthy profit, and still pay you 5% or 6% interest, they must be using your dollars to get a much higher return on the investments they undertake. If they can, so can you.

To repeat. If there's a single answer to "Why isn't everyone rich?" it's that most people don't know how to make money grow. Table 1-1, based on $50 a month or just over $1.66 a day, ought to convince you that $3 a day, properly invested, can spell financial freedom in twenty or thirty years. And it also makes clear that the rate of return on your investment capital is of first importance. The probable rate of return is also the factor over which you have the greatest degree of control.

Plan, Then Pay Yourself First

Most people end up as part of the silent majority—those who lack the means to become secure and independent. There are a number of reasons: maybe they don't know how to hang onto the money they make; or they're too busy paying the finance company to pay themselves first; or they're unwilling to make those small sacrifices today that can lead to a secure tomorrow. Or maybe they simply don't know that it can be done.

You know that it can be done—you've just seen what you're playing for. You've learned that you need a plan, a comprehensive, long-term financial plan that will serve as a framework for your wealth-building program, and will enforce on you the discipline to carry it through. As we develop your plan (we'll be doing that in the next chapter) we'll be considering your financial future in detail. Properly conceived, the plan will serve for years with only minor changes. But you'll have to stick with it to make it work.

That could get tough at times, but remember that your financial future will be riding on it. The fact is, you're going to need a heavy dose of self-discipline to maintain the long-term perspective that is so vital to your wealth-building program. Pressures abound that almost beg you to consume today instead of investing for tomorrow. In large segments of our society, the saving ethic has been thrown out the window, and replaced with a philosophy of "buy now, pay later." Business encourages you to spend more than you make and financial institutions arrange for you to compound your debts on more convenient, and more expensive, terms. You may already know how easy it is to become mired in a swamp of staggering monthly payments—buying, borrowing, buying more, borrowing more. On top of all that, our own government is one of the worst addicts of the "buy now, pay later" approach. Horrendous deficits flow out of Washington year after year, government debt is replaced at maturity with more debt at increasing cost, and inflation cheapens the dollars you earn and save.

With all these pressures on you, it can be almost impossible to discipline yourself, to continue to pay yourself first. It might seem easier to take the path of least resistance, to ride the economic bubble until it bursts. You think, "We'll all be in the same boat, then, won't we? Flat broke." That isn't necessarily so! There will be a few astute investors who bucked the crowd, who continued to exercise discipline in their own financial affairs, and who will have the hard cash available to pick up the pieces at bargain prices after the break! Self-confidence, brains, and the most vital element of all, discipline, are a hard combination to come by, but together they will ensure that you have money on hand when the opportunities are there for the taking.

Learn How to Be Rich

Once you've armed yourself with a sensible financial plan, and you've determined to *pay yourself first* every month for a number of years, you've taken the first step on the road toward accumulating the money you need. What's next? Learning how to keep the money you accumulate. The single most important skill in your wealth-building program is to know how to make your money work and grow for you. Since you're more concerned with your money than anyone else is, you'll probably be a better manager for your funds than anyone else. You can learn the basics of money management—we'll be introducing you to them. You can even master sophisticated techniques if you're interested. Once you've defined your investment objectives and have chosen investment media that are consistent with your needs, we'll explore some of the simpler of the techniques that can build a fortune for you.

In trying to find methods of wealth building that will work in years to come, we'll have to depend on investment media and techniques that have worked well in the past. To a considerable extent, therefore, we'll be assuming that the legal and economic environment of the future will be much as it is today. If we're going to make sacrifices now in order to build future wealth, we'll have to have faith in a continued respect for civil order and the rights of private property.

The impact of inflation on our investments has to be one of our primary concerns in long-term financial planning. In the very long run, our economic system has averaged about $2^{1}/_{2}\%$ inflation per year. Our natural concern with the inflationary erosion of our investment capital should, again, increase the importance we place on seeking a high rate of return on our assets.

That critical factor, the rate of return you can earn, will

mark the difference between success or failure in your investment program. Success will be yours when you earn enough to
compensate for inflation, pay taxes and incidental charges on
the earnings, and still have enough earnings left over to compound your wealth. Any investment that can't earn enough to
pay the taxes and compensate for the effects of inflation loses
a lot of its appeal. Our job now is to learn how to build our
fortune.

Where Are We Going from Here?

This chapter had a single purpose—to indicate my sincere
conviction that you and I can become financially free—secure
and independent. Let's recap the points we've made. The
basic requirements are a *well-conceived plan* for accumulating
wealth, the *discipline* to set aside a few bucks every day, and a
common-sense method for *making your money work* hard for
you. The rest of this book expands on these basic points.

Any kind of planning process involves two dynamics. First,
there is the selection of goals—what do I want? Then there is
the selection of methods—how can I get there? The next
chapter concentrates on the goals. It focuses on those needs
you can foresee and plan for now. (Those contingencies you
are unable to predict can usually be insured against.) If you've
already got it worked out, if you already know how much you
can add to your investment account every day, every month,
every year, if you already know how much you're going to be
worth in five, ten, or twenty years, Chapter 2 is a skip.
Chapter 3, however, is a jewel. It deals with the second biggest
decision you've got to make—after you've decided to pay
yourself first. It asks, what are the risks? What are the rewards? In other words, it discusses the trade-off between how
much you can expect to make and how much of a loss you
may have to take. It explains why most people lose in the investment game, and how you can take advantage of their mas-
ochistic, herd-like habits. It's a minor study in mass psychology, and it lays the groundwork for the investment techniques

that are likely to carry you through to the first twenty or thirty thousand dollars. In short, it copes with that most challenging question of all: How can I get there?

Unless you're interested in the details of compound growth, in a couple of perfectly legal ways to beat the taxman out of $300 to $500 a year, and in ways to have your capital growth tax-deferred, Chapter 4 may be a bit dry. It ends on a promising note, however, with a few guidelines for deciding where to put your money. Chapters 5 and 6 push that point to its extreme, with a battery of historical data that indicate what you and I already know.

If you want to become financially secure, you have to have a piece of the action. That means *ownership*. You've got to own either real estate or common stocks or both. Neither carries a guarantee. In any type of equity situation, there's some chance that you'll lose part or all of your investment capital. But that's exactly why you can expect to earn a higher return in real estate or in common stocks than you would in a bank. You get paid more for accepting the risk of loss. So there are only two ways to go: real estate or common stocks. But unless you've already got twenty or thirty thousand, you've only got one real choice—that's the stock market. For the first twenty or thirty, it's the only game in town.

I hear you now. "So you're suggesting that I find the IBM of the 1980s." Fat chance! Chapter 7 indicates that your chances of pulling that off are about the same as your chances of hitting the Irish Sweepstakes. What then? Chapter 8 starts an explanation of simple formula plans: how to accumulate money, how to protect money, and what's right and what's wrong with the formulas. When we discover their strengths and weaknesses, we can combine their best aspects into a better technique in Chapter 9. Chapters 10 and 11 show you what the betting odds are in the stock market and how to use them to your own advantage. They indicate exactly why we've chosen the method we have, and exactly how to select the best investment vehicle.

Chapter 12, "Does It Work?" is a test of the whole system, put together on $100 a month with $1000 in starting capital, over one of the *worst* decades for the average stock since the

Depression. I wouldn't expect you to listen to another word unless I could offer you evidence of success. And what better evidence than to show you how, in one of the very worst ten-year periods in history, $1000 and $100 a month compounded to nearly $30,000! Sure, there's a remote chance that you'll lose your shirt using this method in the 1980s. But I doubt it. There has never been a ten-year period since the Depression in which you would have suffered that fate. The method takes a little effort—about an hour a week if you're really into it. And you can be sure that it's not the ultimate answer. It's not intended to be. But once you've got the first twenty or thirty thousand, you'll be so involved with the whole investment process you'll spend a good deal of time exploring different methods. Our emphasis here is on a technique to get you the first twenty or thirty thousand in the first ten years. Chapter 12 shows that our technique works.

The last chapter is personal. I got off to a lousy start myself by following the advice of "experts." You can—in fact, you're entitled to—do better. Chapter 13 suggests strongly that you keep your own counsel.

Now let's see where you are today and where you want to be tomorrow.

What's
the Payoff?

O.K., you've decided that you're going to be the one person in fifty who does have enough money to enjoy life. Most of the other forty-nine—those who got lost in the shuffle—probably blew it right at the start *by never starting at all*. At thirty or thirty-five, retirement is only an abstract word—something old people do, but nothing to get concerned about. In your youth it's everything you can do to keep up the car payments, the rent or house payments, and the stereo payments, and still have a little bit left over to play with. The future's a long way off, so why not spend it all now? By your late thirties or early forties, the real impact of the term "financial future" begins to sink in. "Fifteen or twenty years of sweat and toil," you say, "and what have I got to show for it? Still those car payments and house payments, *plus* furniture payments, insurance payments, medical bills, dental bills. Wonder if the kids really need to go to college? And what have I got for myself?"

12

Those are tough questions to be facing at forty. If you're convinced that you can wait to start planning your financial future, that you can push it off a few years down the road, think again. That attitude is why those forty-nine are going to be subsisting on Social Security with maybe—just maybe—a puny pension. Mistake number one is believing that tomorrow is way, way out there. You have to sit down, *today*, now, not tomorrow or next month, and decide three things: *where you are right now; where you want to be* financially at some point in the future; and *how you're going to get from here to there.* This chapter will focus on points one and two.

To provide answers, we'll need a specific listing of your investment goals. *How much* money do you need? *When* will you need it? *For what purposes* will you need it? That list will help you target your financial objectives. Then we'll construct your personal financial inventory—a net worth statement to indicate where you are today, and an income projection to estimate how much money you need to add to your net worth each year. All this should give us a clear picture of your monetary condition. Finally, after we have worked out the goals you want to reach and your starting point, we can develop a strategy for linking the means available (your payments to yourself) to the ends you have chosen.

How Much Money Is Enough?

Let me assure you that the planning process isn't as painful as it sounds. And it's the only way you'll know how you're going to make it. As you probably expected, there's no single answer to "How much money is enough?" Fifty thousand may be enough, or five hundred thousand too little, depending on your own circumstances and desires. The only guideline to your personal "how rich?" decision is the style of living to which you'd like to become accustomed.

Fortunately, your major needs for money fall into two neat classifications: those needs that can be foreseen and thus can be planned for, and those needs that cannot be foreseen but that, in the main, *can* be insured against. It's these unforeseen needs that can wreck even the best of investment programs. The financial consequences of some events can be catastrophic, so it is essential to provide adequate protection against such insurable risks as death, disability, property loss, personal liability, health care, and extended unemployment, before you even begin to concentrate on your wealth-building process. It doesn't take much; a small cash reserve and a well-designed program of insurance coverage will provide sufficient protection against these risks. At this point, I've got to say it loud and clear. *Insurance is not an investment. Insurance is a way to protect yourself against disaster.* And it does. That's why you need it. But although insurance protection takes part of the burden off your shoulders, most *investments* in insurance, by which I mean monies over and above the cost of basic protection, won't earn at a high enough rate of return to make them worth your while. As a general rule, you'll be better off financially if you *buy protection only.* Then invest the difference where you can get a much higher rate of return. You need to make your money work as hard for you as it can, so take every edge you can get.

After you've built a small (and I mean *small*) cash reserve for contingencies and have bought the necessary insurance against catastrophic risks, there are several other needs you can anticipate and plan for. We'll skip the normal provisions for food, clothing, transportation, personal care, and taxes, since they inevitably come from current income. Those items don't require much in the way of long-term planning. What we need to concentrate on are the big-ticket outlays. For instance: where are you going to live? Do the kids really need all that book-learning? These certainly require some consideration now. You're going to have lots of money tied up in these decisions, and you don't want to botch them. Actually, most of these needs are easy to plan for, since you're able to predict when they'll occur. In addition, you can probably foresee other large expenditures for which you need to plan—maybe starting a business of your own, buying a second home, or indulging some costly special interest. But of course the most important, and the most unavoidable, is the provision you'll have to make for retirement.

Once your plan is set up, it will greatly improve the odds that you will have the hard cash available for these specific purposes when it's needed. You may have to make a rather hefty payment to yourself each month to achieve your desired goals. Or you may be able to get by with a very small monthly investment. It all depends on how old you are, how much wealth, or debt, you've already accumulated, and how much you expect to earn over the years. And while I suspect that your lifestyle is probably quite different from that of the average guy, it may be useful to consider his plight for a second. Your own plan will be of the same general structure as his would—or should—be, so let's look at him, just to see how his situation compares with your own present condition.

According to government statistics for 1975 (the latest available), the average family's annual income is about $14,100. They've got a problem, however: they need about $14,600 just to live moderately. So they're falling about $40 behind each month . . . slowly and surely sinking into the morass of monthly payments. Their income statement in Table 2-1 makes it plain.

Here's a head of family who's working himself into the ground, eight hours a day, and he's not saving one red cent. His Social Security tax is likely to triple, and he's already in the

Table 2-1. Net income statement for a typical family, 1975.

Income		$14,100
Expenses		
Food	$3,600	
Housing	3,300	
Transportation	1,200	
Clothing	1,100	
Personal Care	300	
Medical Care	700	
Income Taxes	2,100	
Social Security	800	
Other Items	1,500	
Total Expenses		$14,600
(Deficit)		($500)

Table 2-2. Statement of net worth of a typical worker, 1975.

Assets		Liabilities	
Savings	$ 1,800	Personal Loans	$ 600
Insurance (Cash Value)	4,550	Automobile Loan	1,500
Automobile	3,800	Mortgage on House	14,500
House	37,000	Other	200
Other Assets	6,000		
Total Assets:	$53,150	Total Liabilities:	$16,800
		Net Worth = Assets − Liabilities:	
		($53,150 − $16,800)	$36,350

hole. And as if that weren't enough, he's in his late thirties, he's got two kids, and he's made almost no provision for either their education or his own retirement. About the only thing he's got going for him, as shown in the net worth statement on Table 2-2, is some equity in his house after ten years of mortgage payments, a fairly new car, a small cash value in his $30,000 life insurance policy, and some savings. His personal balance sheet indicates that he has a net worth *today* of about $36,350 after debts of $16,800 are subtracted from assets of $53,150. As for tomorrow, he knows he faces two screaming needs—see Table 2-3.

Table 2-3. Foreseeable needs requiring large outlays*—typical worker, 1975.

Need	Years from Now	Amount per Year	Total Amount
Education			
1st Child	5, 6, 7 & 8	$ 4,000	$ 16,000
2nd Child	8, 9, 10 & 11	4,000	16,000
Retirement	22, 23 . . . 41, 42	14,000*	175,000**

*Assume constant dollars and constant lifestyle.
**Assume 5% earning rate + 8% withdrawal rate at age sixty with an additional twenty-year life expectancy.

With his income statement in Table 2-1, his net worth statement in Table 2-2, and the sketch of his foreseeable needs in Table 2-3, we've got a pretty fair idea of our typical friend's current financial condition. And we can see that he's going to run into some serious problems a few years down the line. Let's see how we'd go about setting up a plan using his situation as an example.

We'll start with the admittedly unrealistic assumption that there will be zero inflation in future years; this lets us work in constant dollars. Just to make it tough, let's also assume that our man will have to provide for his own retirement in his early sixties, and that he'll want no reduction in his material lifestyle. That means he's going to have to come up with $14,000 a year (again, constant dollars) for maybe twenty or more years out of a retirement fund that today has a balance of $0. He'll also have to come up with money for the kids' education. On the basis of the assumptions we've made, and further assuming that he'll last until he's eighty, with his retirement fund safely tucked away in a bank account at 5% interest, we can now schedule his needs (Table 2-4).

As a practical matter, he'll probably qualify for Social Security; he may also be vested in a company-sponsored retirement plan, so he isn't going to be stuck with the job of providing the full amount of his own retirement. On the other hand, despite our complacent assumption, it's not very likely that we'll have *no inflation* in future years. That means that the $14,000 he's counting on for normal living each year may represent considerably less in terms of its actual purchasing power than it does now. Granted all that, we'll still stick with our simplifying assumptions, so that we can concentrate on his major investment needs—those capital requirements for his children's education and his own retirement fund. As you can see, his situation is far from comfortable. In fact, it's grim. It's not a disaster—yet—but you can bet he didn't plan to find himself in this hole.

Naturally, if he had planned for his financial future early on, his prospects could have been very much better. If he had had the foresight to accumulate just $30,000 in his youth, and if he were to invest that money at a 10% annual earning rate until his retirement, *nearly all his future needs would be taken care of,* as you can see from Table 2-5.

But hold it. Don't assume from Table 2-5 that your situa-

Table 2-4. Schedule of foreseeable needs for a typical family, 1975.

Years from Now	Age	Education Child 1	Education Child 2	Withdrawals from Retirement Fund (8% of principal)	Principal in Retirement Fund (Earning 5% interest)
Today	38				
1	39				
.	.				
.	.				
.	.				
5	43	$4,000			
6	44	4,000			
7	45	4,000			
8	46	4,000	$4,000		
9	47		4,000		
10	48		4,000		
11	49		4,000		
.	.				
.	.				$175,000
22	60			$14,000	169,000
23	61			14,000	162,000
24	62			14,000	156,250
25	63			.	.
26	64			.	.
27	65			.	.
.	.			.	.
.	.			.	.
.	.			.	.
41	79			14,000	13,250
42	80			14,000	—

tion is hopeless unless you've managed to save thirty thousand by the time you're forty. That is definitely not the case! What Table 2-5 *does* say, and I hope you're reading it loud and clear if you're in your twenties or early thirties, is that if you can accumulate money early in life, and if you can invest it at a decent rate of return, there's absolutely no reason to worry about your financial future. Time and compounding, given enough of both, will ensure your financial security and independence once you've stashed the first twenty-five or thirty thousand.

Table 2-5. A partial solution to the problem of foreseeable needs ($30,000 invested at 10% at age 38).

Age	Cash Required (Foreseeable Needs)	Earnings on Principal (Net of Cash Required)	Principal Balance
38	—		$ 30,000
39	—	$ 3,000	33,000
40	—	3,300	36,300
41	—	3,630	39,930
42	—	3,993	43,923
43	$ 4,000	4,392 – 4,000 = $392	44,315
44	4,000	4,432 – 4,000 = 432	44,747
45	4,000	4,475 – 4,000 = 475	45,222
46	8,000	4,522 – 8,000 = (3,478)	41,744
47	4,000	4,174 – 4,000 = 174	41,918
48	4,000	4,192 – 4,000 = 192	42,110
49	4,000	4,211 – 4,000 = 211	42,321
50	—	4,232	46,553
.	.	.	.
.	.	.	.
.	.	.	.
.	.	.	.
60	14,000	12,075	132,821

Let's Get Back to You

Now that we've looked at the average guy's situation, got any ideas on what *you* need to do? Let's deal with that question now. Your needs for retirement funding and for the other purposes you can predict depend largely on your own individual circumstances, but let's try to come up with a ballpark figure, an estimate of how large your fortune should be. Again for the sake of simplicity, we'll be referring to *real after-tax* dollars, assuming for the moment no inflation and no taxation. Of course, we'll have to keep in mind that inflation, which has averaged about $2^1/2\%$ per year over the last century, and taxes, which can rip off as much as half of your investment earnings (unless you're careful), are continuously working against you.

Retirement Fund

The size of the retirement fund you'll need to build depends on several factors: when you want to retire, which determines how many years you'll be living on the money; other sources of income you may expect to receive during your retirement years; the earnings rate on your funds once you've retired; and the amount you withdraw to live on each year. For example, if you want to retire at fifty, have no other sources of retirement income, plan to live at the Miami Beach Hilton, and demand the security of a bank for your money, you'll need a huge retirement reserve before you quit. On the other hand, if you plan to retire at sixty-five, have Social Security and/or a vested pension, are satisfied to live frugally, or can earn a high return on your money, you would need only a moderate fund at retirement. Table 2-6 shows the number of years a modest retirement fund of $100,000 (that's right, modest!) will last at various combinations of withdrawal rate and earning rate. Of course, if you can earn money as fast as you withdraw it, you'll never touch the principal and your fund will last forever. Notice, however, that in order to maintain even a moderate lifestyle after retirement, you're somewhat restricted—either you can't retire early, *or* you must have

Table 2-6. Life span of a $100,000 retirement fund.

Withdrawn Each Year	Years Fund Will Last at the Following Earnings Rates					
	5%	*6%*	*7%*	*8%*	*9%*	*10%*
$ 5,000	forever					
6,000	36	forever				
7,000	25	33	forever			
8,000	20	23	30	forever		
9,000	16	18	22	28	forever	
10,000	14	15	17	20	26	forever
11,000	12	13	14	16	19	25
12,000	11	11	12	14	15	18
13,000	9	10	11	12	13	15
14,000	9	9	10	11	11	13
15,000	8	8	9	9	10	11

other sources of income, *or* you must have a very large retirement fund.

Now we'll try to pin down some numbers on the required size of your retirement fund. First, it would be nice to know how many years you had left after you decided to leave work. Table 2-7 shows just about what you can expect, though the numbers will probably improve a bit over the next couple of decades. Didn't know you had so long, did you? Other than the well-established fact that women tend to outlast men, the table simply indicates that you're going to spend a lot of time without a paycheck once you kiss the firm goodbye. Since that's the case, you'd better prepare for it now, unless you have a lot more confidence in the viability and generosity of the Social Security system than I do.

Table 2-7. Life expectancy tables—1975 data.

	Average Years of Life Remaining	
Your Age Now	*Males*	*Females*
25	47	54
30	42	49
35	38	44
40	33	39
45	29	35
50	24	30
55	20	26
60	17	22
65	14	18
70	11	14
75	9	11

Even though Social Security taxes now run higher than income taxes for most people, the Social Security system is run on the "more outgo than income" system the government is so famous for. As it stands right now, there's one taker-out from the system for every three or so payers-in. Consider its condition thirty or forty years from now, when all the postwar babies have reached retirement age, and you can reasonably arrive at the conclusion that those persistent deficits aren't too likely to go away. Since you've been paying and paying into the system all your working life, you're entitled to that nagging question in the back of your mind that asks how much there'll be in the kitty when you're ready to get your share. In any event, Social Security was designed to provide only a minimum living standard—ask anyone who is dependent on it—not as a complete package for enjoying the last quarter of your life. That's not intended to be a scare tactic; it's just a statement of fact. If you want more than the minimum, you're going to have to plan for it.

All right, let's say that you want to retire at fifty-five and you expect to live to be eighty. Your money has to last at least twenty-five years. We'll assume that you'll be entitled to Social Security (maybe $4500 per year on a constant-dollar basis) and a vested company pension (let's use $3500 per year for the purposes of this example). Of course, you'd want to continue to live at least at a moderate level ($15,000 income per year). So you'd need to build a retirement account that would allow you to withdraw $7000 per year (the $15,000 living requirement less the combined income from your $4500 Social Security payment and your $3500 pension) for your final twenty-five years. At that point in your life you won't have much time to make up any money you lose, so you would probably opt for a very low-risk savings account that might earn 5%. Under these circumstances, you'd need a fund of exactly $100,000 to provide additional income.

How do we work that out? Go back to Table 2-6. Find the column that corresponds to the expected earning rate, 5%. In that column, find the number 25, the number of years your fund has to last. Then read left to find the amount you can withdraw each year from a $100,000 fund: $7000.

I hear you again: "Hold on there! Do you mean I've got to have $100,000 on my own, in addition to Social Security and my pension, just to stay at a moderate lifestyle? You're putting me on!" No, I'm not. I wish I were, but you've just read the numbers. And it could be worse.

Now let's keep everything as is, except that this time we'll change one factor—you won't be getting the company pension of $3500 each year. In that unfortunate situation, you'd need a fund from which you could withdraw $10,500 per year

($15,000 income less $4500 from Social Security). Remember that if your $100,000 fund is to last twenty-five years, you can withdraw only $7000 a year. But you need $10,500—1$^1/_2$ times that amount ($10,500/$7000 = 1.5). So *now* you need a retirement fund that is 1$^1/_2$ times the hundred thousand. You need $150,000. And if the worst happened and you were also without Social Security, you'd have to draw the full annual $15,000 from the fund. At only 5% for twenty-five years, you'd need at retirement close to $215,000 ($15,000/$7000 = 2.15) just to go on without a material collapse in your standard of living.

So set your financial goals, but set them realistically. Try to envision your lifestyle as you want it to be, and then try to estimate the income you'll need to maintain that lifestyle (in today's dollars, since we'll consider the effects of inflation and taxes later). Set down when you want to retire, and then note how many years of wealth building you have left. Estimate how long your retirement fund must sustain you, and the rate at which it will earn. As we've said, since you won't want to take too many chances at that age, the savings bank rate of around 5% or so might be a good guess. Then, considering other potential sources of income, determine how much money you need to accumulate for your retirement. That figure is a major goal for which you must plan *now!* Set up a separate account for your investments, pay into it every month before you pay anyone else, and learn how to make it grow. You can be rich or, at the absolute minimum, very comfortable if you've planned for it *and if you'll stick to your plan.*

Other Funds

Even more than the funding requirements for retirement, the funds you establish for purposes such as education, housing, and special interests are very much a matter of personal circumstance. Increasingly, couples are deciding to forgo child-raising (or marriage for that matter) so that both partners can work, can play together, and so on. Obviously, this leads to activities and lifestyles that may require very individual treatment of financial needs. All this is to say that while we can generalize about the need to build a fund for retirement, it's virtually impossible to draw similar generalizations about funds for other specific purposes.

You ought to be able to identify and anticipate how much money you're going to need for purposes other than normal living and you should begin now to plan for and account for these uses separately. Try to look into the future—ask yourself when you need money and what you need it for—foresee your needs and plan for them.

Your Financial Inventory: Get Started on It Now

In the description of the financial condition of our average friend, we used three primary planning tools: a schedule of foreseeable needs, which specified *how much, when,* and *for what* the money was needed; a personal balance sheet, which listed his assets, his liabilities, and the difference between them, or his net worth; and an income statement, which listed all major items of income and expense, with any net (unused) income left over for investment purposes. We'll be using the same tools to plan for you, along with a series of projected net income statements.

Note that a *balance sheet* specifies one's net worth at some specific point in time (for example, December 31, 1978), and that an *income statement* represents the flow of money into and out of one's hands over a period of time. Let's assume that *your* balance sheet on December 31, 1978 (Table 2-8) contained assets worth $50,000 and liabilities of $20,000, leaving you with a net worth of $30,000. If, during 1979, your total income exceeds your total expenses by $2000, then your net

Table 2-8. Balance sheets and income statements.

Balance Sheet December 31, 1978		*Income Statement January–December, 1979*			*Balance Sheet December 31, 1979*	
Assets	$50,000	Income	$15,000		Assets	$52,000
Liabilities	20,000	Expenses	13,000		Liabilities	20,000
Net Worth	$30,000	+ Net Income	$ 2,000	=	Net Worth	$32,000

worth at the end of 1979 should have increased by $2000 (to $32,000) if nothing else has changed.

All right. You've got the tools. Now it's time to scratch out the first draft of your own situation. Take out pencil and paper and give it a shot right now before you forget how to use those tables. Start with the assumption that you will have accumulated $20,000 or so ten years from now, and see if your financial future doesn't look a little more promising than the average.

Schedule of Foreseeable Needs

In the process of determining your foreseeable needs, make yourself think far into the future. Try to specify exactly how much money you will need for every major purpose, and when you think you'll need it. Some job, isn't it, having to give detailed thought to your long-term lifestyle? But it's the basis of your entire financial plan. And what does it tell you? Essentially it tells you that, within reason, anything that you anticipate far enough in advance and for which you're willing to invest regularly can be achieved. No, you probably won't become a multi-millionaire on an average salary. But you can do better than you realize. So in trying to assess your needs, be realistic but don't be stingy. Remember my famous $3 a day? If you're willing to invest just that—just $3 a day—and if you can earn a return of 10% compound annually, you can build a veritable fortune (Table 2-9) *if you're young enough.* That's right! You can wind up with close to half a million dollars by

Table 2-9. Wealth built on $3 per day at 10% return.

Your Age Now	At Age							
	30	35	40	45	50	55	60	65
25	$6,685	$17,450	$34,790	$62,715	$107,690	$180,120	$296,860	$464,685
30		6,685	17,450	34,790	62,715	107,690	180,120	296,860
35			6,685	17,450	34,790	62,715	107,690	180,120
40				6,685	17,450	34,790	62,715	107,690
45					6,685	17,450	34,790	62,715

age sixty-five—if you start early enough—*on an investment of about $90 a month*. No, we haven't considered either taxes or inflation, but there are perfectly legal ways to defer taxes so that your wealth can build on schedule. And there are methods that can raise the rate of return so you can beat, or at least compensate for, inflation. We'll talk about these in later chapters. For the time being, suffice it to say that there is no need to dread retirement.

Statement of Net Worth

On track so far—you've filled out a schedule of foreseeable needs and come up with a number . . . a big number that looks intimidating, maybe even impossible. But *you've got a goal* and goal setting is the first step in the planning process. Now we need to look at your current financial condition to see where you're starting from. Remember that your balance sheet reflects only your condition at some particular point in time. Any investments you make out of your current income, as well as any earnings you garner on those investments, will expand your net worth on the next balance sheet. So even a zero net worth isn't bad for starters. What counts is how much time you've got to build in.

On one side of your balance sheet, try to list all your assets—everything you own or have claim to. Try to segregate them into categories of need. In other words, if you've got $2000 in a checking account, list it, and then consider the reason for its existence. Is it an emergency fund? A vacation fund? Then consider how much it should be. Is $2000 too much? Too little? It's extremely hard to generalize about these things. A lot of people discover they have far too much money tied up in checking accounts, where it earns nothing, in savings account and insurances, where it earns relatively little, and in other places where it isn't working hard enough or it isn't giving them any enjoyment. In my opinion, there are only two reasons for hanging on to any asset. Either you're enjoying its use today, or you're letting it earn money so you can have an even greater amount at some time in the future. With the single exception of a small checking account for day-to-day transactions, if I had an asset that wasn't earning for tomorrow or providing some benefit today, I'd sell it and use the proceeds to buy something that did one or the other.

On the other side of the ledger, list all your debts, the claims others have on your assets or income, and classify them according to when they come due. As you know, short-term unsecured debts, such as those you run up on your credit cards, are extremely expensive—18% per year in some cases. And they cost you a lot more than you could make on the money if you invested it well. That's how the banks can afford to pay you 5% or 6% of your savings, cover all their costs, and still turn a respectable profit. They're investing your savings (which cost them 5% or so) and loaning them out at 18%, and that's not a bad bargain. One of your first duties, then, even before you undertake a major investment program, is to focus your attention and efforts on reducing or completely eliminating those expensive short-term debts. In other words, if you're in hock, get out . . . you're paying too much for the use of their money.

On the other hand, the mortgage on your house and some of your other long-term debts may be relatively inexpensive compared to what you could expect to earn on alternative investments, especially after you consider the tax advantages and the effects of inflation. So if you're carrying a large mortgage on your house, you can relax, especially if, as has been the long-term trend, property values remain stable or generally rise.

Now you have two sides to your ledger. The difference between them—the difference between what you own and what you owe—is your net worth. After you cull out those assets that aren't earning for tomorrow or being enjoyed today, after you sell them off, and after you've eliminated all the expensive short-term plastic-money financing, that net-worth figure is going to be your focal point. In a financial scheme, it's your scorecard in the game of fortune. Net worth, in short, is the measure of your *financial* success.

Projection of Net Income

Projecting your income and your expenses is no more than the familiar process of budgeting. The problem is, however, that lots of people have a strange habit of overlooking their long-term needs in the budgeting process, and as a consequence, they never get around to building any wealth. To avoid the tragedy of living from paycheck to paycheck for the rest of your life, you've got to *include your own future in your current budget and pay yourself* just as you would budget money for food, clothing, shelter, and insurance.

Again, there are no hard and fast rules on how much you should set aside for investment purposes. A big part of that decision depends on how much money you'll need in the future and how many years you have left to accumulate it. As a practical matter, the amount of your monthly investment in your financial freedom should compete on an even basis with every other expense—transportation, personal care, medical care, recreation, education, and so on—after the requirements for food, clothing, shelter, and insurance have been met. Once you have decided on the specific amount you can afford, the vital point is to stick to it. *Never, never fail to give your own future top priority!*

Plan—from Today to Tomorrow

So let's see where we are. After some numerical exercise, you've been able to project your needs for retirement and other major outlays, you've determined your present financial condition, and you've figured out how much you can invest each month. All that's left is to link these parts together by constructing a series of net worth statements that will describe your financial condition at various points in the future. To link the parts into an overall financial plan, it's easier to begin near the end of one's life span and work back toward the here and now.

Picture yourself thirty, forty, fifty or more years from

now. Obviously, when you die, you want to leave an estate that will cover the expenses of your death and perhaps leave a little something behind. So your final balance sheet might look something like this:

Assets	
Savings	$10,000
Other	50,000
Total Assets	$60,000
Liabilities	50,000
Net Worth	$10,000

Now flash back to when you retired twenty years before. You were entitled to Social Security and a company pension which together provided a total of $750 per month for life. But since you had never been enthusiastic about going hungry, you had decided in your youth that retirement should be a reward, not a struggle for survival. In your working years, you were willing to build a fund that would provide an extra $1000 each month for the twenty years following your retirement. Since you didn't want to take any big risks with your money at retirement, you were satisfied to put it into a nice, safe savings account at 5% interest.

Now let's check back to Table 2-6. We see that a $100,000 fund invested at 5% allows you to withdraw $8,000 per year for twenty years. But you want $12,000 per year—$1\frac{1}{2}$ times that amount. So you need a fund that is $1\frac{1}{2}$ times $100,000, or $150,000. Just to keep the next of kin happy, let's assume you want to leave $10,000 for them to remember you by. So your total retirement fund has to be about $160,000. At a minimum, therefore, your projected balance sheet at retirement, with twenty years ahead of you, should have looked something like this:

Assets	
Investments	$160,000
Other	50,000
Total Assets	$210,000
Liabilities	50,000
Net Worth	$160,000

To fulfill your minimum requirements at retirement, you had to have built up a $160,000 stake during your working years.

Just for the sake of argument, we'll say you were thirty when you first began thinking about retirement but you goofed around until you were thirty-five before you finally did something about it. At that point, you decided to give up one or another expensive bad habit, and you were lucky enough to be able to invest the money at a 10% return. Since you only had twenty-five years left until your target retirement age of sixty, you knew that you'd have to do one of two things to reach your goal of $160,000: invest a little more than $3 a day for twenty-five years, or get more than a 10% return. We can see from Table 2-9 that $3 a day for twenty-five years at 10% compounds to $107,690. But you needed $160,000—about 1¹/₂ times that amount. So you had to contribute 1¹/₂ times the $3 each day or about $4.50 . . . either that or earn a higher return. Then, assuming you were starting at absolute zero when you began the program, you could have projected a series of pro-forma balance sheets for each year. By using that procedure—by forecasting balance sheet positions over a series of years—you can ensure that you'll be making ample provision for any of the needs you foresee—retirement, education, special interests, whatever.

To Sum It All Up

If I seem to repeat myself, it's because I happen to think it can't be said too often. The most important factor in becoming wealthy is your attitude. If you know that you're going to be wealthy, the chances are good that you will be. And the *first step in knowing is to have a plan of action* and to be willing to follow through. Financial planning, like planning of any kind, requires that you look into the future. If you can foresee the major financial needs you'll encounter in the future, and if you plan for them now, you're about ninety percent along in answering the question, "How much money is enough?" Your personal balance sheet, using net worth as the key figure, is your guide to how well you are doing. And remember that the larger the monthly investments you're willing to make out of current income, the longer the period of time you have left to earn, and the higher the rate of return you get on your investments, the greater your final wealth will be.

Making Your Money Work Hard

NOW that you've drawn up a good financial plan for your future, you can concentrate on that key figure—net worth. Those additions you've resolved to make every month to your investment account are the basis for compounding your net worth. We've already seen the improvement we make in our investment results by getting a high rate of return. None of us should be willing to settle for any investment that doesn't make our money really *work*. Keep this comparison in mind: $3 a day for twenty years builds to $36,200 if it's invested at 5%, to $62,700 if it's invested at 10%, to $113,100 at 15%, and to $204,400 at 20%. That's one hell of a big difference! It's not easy to get 10% to 15% or more, but it's not impossible either. You have to know where to put your money and how to manage it. But before we jump into the questions of where and how, let's look at some of the more important risks you're going to face in the investment process.

Is There a Guaranteed Highest Rate?

Obviously, the best place in the world for your money would be an investment that offered both a guarantee against capital loss and the highest return available anywhere. Equally obviously, that animal just doesn't exist. As a practical matter, there's no way to get a high return without accepting some chance of loss, so you'll have to decide which investment risks you can handle. You'll also have to decide whether you've got the capacity to manage your own investments successfully. Let's discuss those subjects in reverse order. A short word first on your capacity to do it yourself, followed by a lengthy discussion on your odds of winning or losing in the investment game.

Frankly, if you've got a few hours a month and a strong interest in money, you'll probably do a better job of running your investments than most of the professional money managers would. Unless they're exceptional, the "experts" aren't as interested in your money as you are. To them you're an account number, and a few thousand bucks isn't worth their devoted attention. So you have almost no choice—you'll have to do it yourself. Since you're stuck with the job anyway, it makes sense to learn a few of the basic techniques. And the most important rule is to *do your own thinking!*

Always keep your own counsel. If there's one failing that dooms any investment program, however well designed it may be, it's the temptation to join the thoughtless emotionalism of the crowd. The only way to avoid catastrophe, and wind up making a few dollars on the side, is to do your own thinking. That means you'll be bucking the majority opinion most of the time. It also means you'll be less exposed to disaster when it strikes, and better prepared for opportunity when it arises. The reality is that most individual investors, and many professional money managers as well, swing back and forth between emotional extremes: they get greedy when it's obvious that everything is going well; and they get scared when it's obvious that everything is going bad. *Responding to the obvious is one of the primary causes of dismal investment performance.* If you can keep your head while everyone around you is going crazy on

some speculative bubble—tulips or gold or chinchillas or whatever—if you can maintain a degree of calm when everyone
around you is paralyzed by some ominous dread—military
confrontation or economic collapse or hyperinflation—you've
got it made. *Think, don't react,* and you'll be your own best
money manager. You'll get much higher returns with much
lower risk as a result of your independence.

What Goes Up Must Come Down

I just slipped the whole method for your wealth-building
program into that last paragraph. Since they happen to form
the basis of the technique we're going to use to acquire wealth,
let's spend a few minutes talking about speculation, emotions,
and cycles.

Investment assets are a bit different from other kinds of
assets in that they're subject to periodic bouts of speculation
that can have an important effect on their prices. Let me first
try to draw the distinction between the value of an asset and
its price. Your car is an asset. It's useful because it takes you
where you want to go. Your house is an asset. It's useful because you can live in it and enjoy its comforts. Your ten shares
of AT&T are an asset. They're useful because they pay you a
dividend with which you can buy enjoyment. There's also a
slight speculative element there, because the price of those ten
shares goes up and down without any necessary relation to
their underlying value. Now, how about your five hundred
shares of South Colombian Mining Company? Or your forty
acres of California desert? Purely speculative assets—with no
current usefulness; you're holding them because you hope
that someday somebody is going to give you more for them
than you paid.

Obviously, there are a lot of shades of grey in the distinction between a useful asset and a speculative asset. Actually,
it's more a matter of what motivates people to buy or sell the
asset than the inherent usefulness of the asset itself. There is
absolutely no reason why a useful asset like your house
couldn't become the subject of rampant speculation, and there

are houses that have become precisely that. Nor is there any reason why an inherently useless asset like the forty acres of Mojave Shores couldn't be completely ignored by speculators. The speculative distinction depends on people's motives for buying or selling.

In discussing the difference between value and price, let's use common stocks as an example, since more mini-speculators have been burned in the stock market than anywhere else. But keep in mind that the same thinking applies to almost any asset in which you're likely to have money invested—antique cars, stamp collections, gold coins, real estate, common stocks, original editions, classic comics, baseball cards, art, precious gems—almost any investment other than a savings account. The fact is, there can be a wide gap between the value of an asset as determined by its usefulness and its price.

"Hold it!" you say. "Slow down. What are you saying? What's all this price/value stuff? Aren't they the same thing?" No, most emphatically not. In fact, they can be and frequently are very different things. If I haven't made the difference clear, I'd better try again. Because this is crucial.

For our purposes, let's describe the *value* of an asset as what it's worth as a useful entity. That still doesn't make sense? Let's try your house as an example. All the houses on your block are identical in every respect; you did a little checking and found they all rent for around $300 a month, so you are willing to pay $300. O.K., what's the house worth? Well obviously, its value *in use* is $300 a month. Now let's translate that into a fair value. Keep in mind now, we're not discussing its price, which might be entirely different.

Experience over many years has shown that typical houses in typical neighborhoods have normally sold at between 80 and 120 times their monthly rental, or their fair value in use. By then applying the historical standard to the $300 rental, you can arrive at a figure of $24,000 to $36,000 as the fair value of the house. If your standard of value has been taken over a long enough period of time to include both the best and the worst of historical experience, it's a pretty reliable guide. That figure may or may not have much in common with the prevailing market price; it's simply what has been considered fair value in the past. Now let me ask you a question. Would you *now* buy that house for $25,000? For $40,000? For $65,000? We'll discuss that in Chapter 6.

Back to the stock market, where most people end up getting their brains rattled and their accounts emptied fast, and where, with the exception of the commodities market, you find the most consistent example of speculative excess. The greed/fear syndrome is certainly not confined to stocks—real estate booms, gold fevers, and tulip manias are among the classics, and I was personally fortunate enough to witness a canary craze in the Orient in the mid-60s. But speculative cycles do seem to run through the stock market at somewhat regular intervals of about three to six years. Thus, the stock market is a useful example simply because it offers so many speculative cycles to observe and work with.

Now your big question still is: how can there be a difference between price and value? The answer is this. If everyone knew the standards of real value and if everyone were completely rational, there wouldn't be much difference between the two. Price and value should be the same. But because most people don't know or care about the standards of value, and because they don't or won't act rationally, there is usually a significant difference between the price they're willing to pay and the fair value of what they're buying. And there's your key. I said that you'd spend most of your time bucking the crowd, and that's the reason. If you're smart, you'll be guided by long-observed standards of value, even when the majority has thrown them aside as "no longer true in today's new environment." You'll trust your own judgment no matter how fevered or panicked others may be. If you do, you will profit mightily from their recurring delirium.

But how, you wonder, can they do it to themselves? Remember Economics I? Remember microeconomics, supply and demand, and all that other marginal stuff? Let's drag out the Law of Supply and Demand and see if we can discover why the crowd insists on cremating itself time and time again. To get us all started at the same spot, let's give the basics a quick review.

First, demand. Basic point: reduce the price, and people

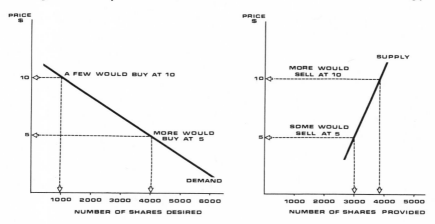

Chart 3-1. Demand and supply.

will buy more of a given product or service. Look at Chart 3-1. Demand appears as a curve sloping downward and to the right when it is drawn the way the economists do. Supply goes in the opposite direction, so we can expect it to rise. Suppliers, that is, will usually provide more of something as the price they can get goes up. Now let's plot these two curves together as in Chart 3-2. What do you get where those lines cross? Market price, that price at which the quantity supplied by

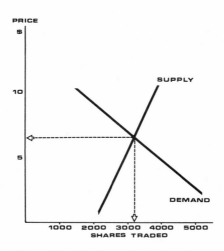

Chart 3-2. Market price and volume.

sellers exactly equals the quantity demanded by buyers—equilibrium. What could conceivably change that?

Well, we know that the downward slope of the demand curve is determined by the fact that people can afford more at low prices and less at high prices. But what about the absolute level of the demand curve? What if they don't want any of the stuff at any price? That normally occurs in an undervalued (prices lower than true value on an historic "fair value" basis) market as shown in Chart 3-3—regardless of the bargain, no one is interested! Or they're scared. What if they want tremendous quantities of it regardless of price? The huge speculative demand supports market prices well above the historic norm (see Chart 3-4), because everyone is excited. Or they're greedy. Now we've got a second factor in the picture, an underlying factor that's just as important as the price/quantity trade-off. What really determines the level of demand for stocks? People's expectations, their enthusiasm, or lack of same.

When people become optimistic about the future, their demand for common stocks, as well as other speculative assets, rises in proportion. The increased demand causes the market price to rise. The cycle of expanding confidence and rising prices can repeat itself only so often before it attracts specula-

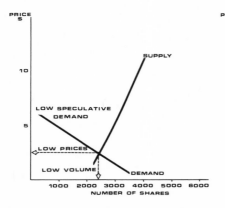

Chart 3-3. An undervalued market: low speculative demand, low prices, low volume.

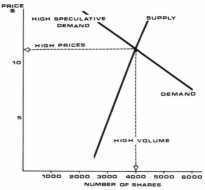

Chart 3-4. An overvalued market: high speculative demand, high prices, high volume.

tors. Before long people's thinking, or lack of it, changes from reasonable expectations of improved economic conditions to overblown hopes of never-ending prosperity. The two common characteristics of this transition from normal demand to speculative demand are, first, a succession of "good-news" announcements, plausible explanations that tend to confirm the early price rises, and second, the public's increasing suspicion that "something's going on there."

That's when the skyrocket effect sets in. Before too many rounds of speculators have moved in, the market begins to move out of its normal area of fair value and into an area of overvaluation. Every step in the upward trend depends on the entry of newer, and usually less astute, speculators, as well as on continued bursts of "good-news." The smart money knows when prices have moved out of line; when the value yardstick has been left behind, rational investors stop buying. And so, increasing numbers of new speculators are needed to keep demand expanding and prices rising. At the same time, continuing confirmations in heavier and heavier doses are needed to attract the next new round of speculators. In the final hours of the uptrend, there will be very few real investors left in the market, just a wildly optimistic mob of little guys who are out to make a killing by playing "greater fool" with their hard-earned money. Eventually, everybody who wanted a piece of the action has put his last buck on the line. There's no more money left on the sidelines to propel prices any higher, and the market has attracted the last remaining greater fool. It's hanging like a snowbank on a mountainside. And the only question left is, when is it going to fall, and how hard?

Let me show you a series of numbers: 17, 20, 23, 26, 29, 32, 34, 36. What's the trend? Right. Another series: 38, 40, 42, 43, 44. Same trend direction, slowing down but still steady. Again: 45, 44, 45, 46, 45, 44, 45, 46. Now there's no way to identify the trend, is there? Question: Suppose you'd gotten into this market for a two-year ride from the low 20s, and you'd chalked up thousands of dollars worth of paper gains. With a shapeless trend like that, how long would you hang around waiting for it to tack on a couple of points more? Not long.

And neither would the other smart speculators. They

know the market's become ridiculously overvalued. They've got fat paper profits to protect, so they're ready to run for cover before the market gives them an *obvious reason* to duck. Now all the smart guys are selling. And that adds to supply, which forces prices down, and that scares the next smallest round of speculators. They too start selling, adding more new supply, creating faster price drops, and the avalanche is on. There's no way to tell exactly where it tops out until after the fact. But there are telltale signs that ought to warn you when you stand a greater chance of losing your shirt than of making a killing. The three common characteristics of the peak in a speculative cycle are these: First, the market is grossly over-valued on the basis of any reasonable historic standard. Second, there are so many "good-news" announcements, people have convinced themselves that this is just the beginning of the ride. And third, the public has jumped in with both feet because the market has been going up for years.

How long, how deep, or how bloody the inevitable washout will be is next to impossible to predict. Round after round of dismayed mini-speculators will be forced to dump their broken dreams onto the market for whatever prices they can get before the slide runs its course. Later on, there will be a long string of bad-news shots that lets them know just what went wrong. Until finally things reverse themselves. The market becomes as grossly undervalued near the bottom as it was overvalued at the top. The evening news is so bad that almost everyone thinks the world is coming to an end; complete collapse of the economic system is a typical prognostication. And the masses wouldn't touch stocks with a ten-foot pole because the market has been crashing for years.

But there will be a few smart investors out there who will grab the chance to pick up bargains at below fair value. And they will have the cash to do the buying. They're the guys who folded out of the game near the top.

Are There Other Investment Risks?

Now you know about the biggest risk, the speculative cycle. Let's look at some of the others.

Investment, as opposed to speculation or gambling, involves the *considered acceptance of higher risks (which already exist) in exchange for the expectation of higher returns.* For example, when you decide to move your money from a savings account (which has almost no risk of capital loss) into high-grade bonds (where there's some chance of loss, since the corporation could go belly-up before the bonds mature), you would do so only if you expected to earn a higher return. In the classic sense, you would be investing: You would have taken a long-term perspective and you would be mentally prepared to hold the bonds until they mature. The speculator, on the other hand, would buy those bonds without intending to hold them to maturity. Instead, on the basis of his analysis of money market conditions, he may be anticipating a general fall in interest rates, and a corresponding price rise for the bonds. Because his investment horizon (how long he plans to hold the asset) is shorter, he is subject to greater risk, since bond prices could collapse, but he has the prospect of greater rewards if his analysis is correct.

Now it would be downright idiotic to accept the risk of loss if you weren't getting paid extra for doing it. Yet gamblers persist in accepting artificially created risks, where the odds are almost invariably against the player, on the faintest hopes of great gains. Sure, it's *possible* to win a fortune by gambling, but it's a virtual *certainty* that you can build a fortune by investing. Invest or speculate against the crowd, but don't gamble—and don't take any risks you don't get paid for!

We talked about the acceptance of risk. With most types of worthwhile investment, there is the chance that you could lose part of your capital. By their very nature, investments in real estate, stocks, bonds, and mortgages are more subject to actual capital loss than are investments in savings accounts or insurance contracts. As a natural result, these riskier investments have to yield higher long-term returns in order to attract capital. If you're willing to accept and deal with those risks, you've got a better chance of becoming rich. But *safety of your investment capital should be the primary objective for your dollars in the area of investment.*

There's another aspect of the problem of investment losses, one many investors tend to overlook. Suppose you've been given the opportunity to invest in asset A, where you can earn a return of 12%. But you choose for some reason to put your money into asset B, which has exactly the same degree of risk but which earns only 8%. Not too swift! You've just given up the opportunity to earn an extra 4% per year with the same exposure to loss. Four percent doesn't sound like too much. But the difference (it's called opportunity loss) would amount to $140,000 lost—tossed away—over thirty years on your $90 per month. So it's imperative to arrive at a proper balance between the chance of actual capital loss and the chance of missing out on some more profitable opportunity. And in spite of my warning on safety, I'd advise you to tip the balance toward profitability rather than safety while you're still young.

Sources of risk apply both to actual loss (when the market price of your investment is going down) and to opportunity loss (when the price of other investments is rising more rapidly than yours). There are several kinds of risk to which your investments will be exposed.

First, there's what's known as *specific risk*. That's the chance you took when you bought several homesites in Rattlesnake City, purchased a hundred shares of Penn Central stock, invested in New York City bonds, or bought a house which is now occupied by the local contingent of Hell's Angels. Specific risk is the chance that your investment will go down in price while other investments are retaining their value or going up. In other words, it's the chance that you'll choose the one that bombs. Specific risk applies to one unit or small group of units (that one house or neighborhood, that one company or industry, or that one issuer or class of issuer), and it can cause changes in investment value that are not related to the established markets for similar investments. The problem of specific risk arises when you have to decide which particular stock to buy if you're in the stock market, or which income unit to buy if you're in real estate.

Fortunately, there is an easy and complete answer to the problems created by specific risk: diversification. Diversification means that you invest in many different assets, not just in one or a few. That means lots of individual pieces of real estate, or lots of individual stocks, or lots of individual bonds, or lots of individual mortgages. Diversification is based on the theory that the good surprises will cancel out the bad, that one high flyer will more than make up for one absolute disaster. It sounds almost too simple, but it works! The overwhelming evidence indicates that sufficient diversification will almost completely eliminate specific risk. Just as important, the evidence indicates that you don't get paid extra for accepting specific risk. So unless you are already, or can soon become, an expert, it's a whole lot smarter to simply diversify your investments and get rid of the entire problem. Even the experts use diversification as a hedge against making the wrong selection. And so should you!

Go ahead. Say it. "Come on, Hayes, what about me and my $90 a month, big shooter? How am I going to diversify?" Since it would be a pretty neat trick to run out and buy a diversified group of apartment buildings on $3 a day, you'll probably have to scratch real estate for a few years unless you've already got big bucks to begin with. Same holds true for mortgages, since they usually start at a few thousand dollars each and run up from there. Both media offer some real advantages, but not for people who are just starting their wealth building.

That leaves us with stocks and bonds as the logical place to put our money. "So I should go out and buy a quarter-share of IBM or a tenth of a bond every month?" No, you don't need one stock or one bond. You need lots of stocks and/or lots of bonds. You need twenty or thirty different issues to eliminate specific risk. And you *do* want to eliminate it, since you earn nothing for accepting specific risk. "Don't tell me! You're not going to suggest a mutual fund, are you?" Yep, I am. Now hang on and let me tell you why.

Mutual funds, which pool your investment capital along with the investments of other people, provide the diversification you've got to have. "Don't put me on. I had an uncle in Moline who bought a mutual fund and he's really taken a bath on it." O.K., that may be true, but only because he didn't buy it right. Mutuals do go down, but they also go up. Fortunately, mutual funds do just what the stock market does, and that's exactly what you need. Mutual funds offer the unique advantage of allowing you to hold a well-diversified portfolio for $90 a month or less. There's simply no other high-return media you can get into for $3 a day!

On the average, mutual funds offer about the same return as the stock market and they can be bought without any commission! That's known as a no-load mutual fund. And that's important. Don't *ever* pay a sales commission to buy your fund shares: there's virtually no difference in investment performance between the typical load fund, which may charge up to $8^3/_4\%$ just to get in, and a no-load fund, which doesn't charge any sales commission. The point is, your no-load mutual fund operates in an investment market where you can expect to earn at least 9% or 10% per year over the long haul. And if your fund is bought right, you'll do a lot better than 9% or 10% a year. We'll see about that later. By the way, almost all mutual fund salesmen will try to sell you on the value of "professional management," but you shouldn't take that too seriously. You need the diversification more than you need their expertise. And a fund gives you the necessary diversification in amounts you can afford.

So you're covered against specific risk if you invest your $90 a month in a diversified no-load mutual fund. What happens then? Your fund *will go up,* and your fund *will go down*— and that's another form of risk: market risk. Market risk is the chance that your investments will change in value even when there is no apparent reason for them to do so. The stock market is an auction and, like any other auction, prices are determined by what buyers are willing to pay (demand) and by what sellers are willing to take (supply). That's the speculative cycle we talked about. When people are happy, and greedy, they'll be willing to shell out a lot more dollars for stocks than they're really worth. And prices will soar as the cycle moves toward a top. Sooner or later, something always happens to douse the speculative fires, and prices plummet even more rapidly than they climbed. Eventually, everyone will be so gloomy about prospects for the future that they'll gladly sell the same shares back to you for a fraction of their true value.

Market risk is your tool! Because of market risk, the prices of all securities fluctuate up and down, just as will the share price of your mutual fund. Because security prices move up and down so rapidly, there's a lot more room for profit when you buy and sell your fund intelligently. So you're going to learn to take advantage of market risk by knowing how to recognize when prices have been driven too far above their worth on waves of speculative greed, or when prices have been driven too far below their worth by fear and panic. Once you do, if you can stick to your own counsel, you'll have the best money manager around.

In order to take advantage of those recurring cycles in securities prices, you'll want to do two things. First, make sure your investments are highly marketable. Unlike real estate and mortgages, both of which are relatively illiquid, you can buy or sell your mutual fund shares on very short notice at the prevailing market price (their net asset value). That's a nice bonus. You don't have to worry about the hefty commissions or discounts from prevailing market price you might face if you tried to dump real estate on the market in a hurry, nor about the huge mark-down you'd face in peddling a mortgage.

The second step you'll take is just as important. It's essential to hold some portion of your investment capital in the form of a cash-equivalent reserve at all times. This will ensure that you've got the money you need to take advantage of special opportunities as they present themselves. You never know when the bargains will appear, but they will, sooner or later. And as we'll see, you'll get a greatly increased rate of return if you've got the hard cash to grab a bargain on those rare occasions when everyone else wants out.

And now we come to the last of the risks we face in investing. The overall condition of the money markets is going to be very important to your investment success, so we're going to study those markets and learn how to use them to our benefit. Investments in bonds, mortgages, and, to a lesser extent, common stocks are subject to price changes caused by changes in the prevailing interest rates. Usually, the prices of these securities move in a direction opposite to that of interest rates. For example, a decline in the prevailing interest rate usually sparks a rally in the bond market and in the stock market.

You'll get extra profits by tracking the money markets and your mutual fund closely, so watch them like a hawk.

Summary: Dealing with Risk

But you ask, couldn't I avoid all this risk and do just as well in other forms of investment? The answer is no. Almost all investments are subject to the loss of purchasing power through continued inflation. Cash, savings accounts, insurances, bonds, and mortgages are especially vulnerable. Between the eroding effects of inflation and the confiscatory effects of higher taxation by all levels of government, most fixed income investments have done rather poorly over the years. And the possible loss of purchasing power through taxation and inflation is something you have to consider in your long-term planning. Unless you expect a major change in government attitudes toward inflation and taxation, fixed income investments probably won't be suitable for your wealth-building program.

The fact is, the whole process of plunking your money down and making it work for you *involves taking some risks.* I've pointed out that you can deal with *specific* risk easily enough: buy a well-diversified no-load mutual fund and eliminate the "which?" problem altogether. A no-load mutual fund is the easiest and cheapest way to acquire diversification and, if you've got less than $10,000 or $20,000 dollars to start with, it's about the only high-earning investment medium you can afford.

There's no way, however, around *market* risk and *interest-rate* risk. You'll have to accept both if you want to earn more than a miser's rate of return on your investments. The opportunity loss in most alternatives is so great that you have to invest where you can expect to earn at least 9% or 10% per year. And there's only one place that a beginning investor can reasonably expect to get 9% or more: in the stock market.

And we'll soon see that there's a way to turn speculative market cycles to our advantage so that we can earn much higher rates of return.

Money,
More Money,
and
Even More Money!

NOW'S the time to dream a little bit, to contemplate that bundle of cash. How big will it grow? The working principle in wealth building is *compounding*. For example, say that you put $1 into an investment that returns 10% per year to you. Assuming your returns are tax-free, you'll have $1.10 at the end of the first year: your original $1 + $0.10 return. During the second year, the entire $1.10 will earn a 10% return ($0.11) and you'll have $1.21 by the end of the second year. The money you earned during the first year will have earned additional returns during the second year—money earned on the money you earned the year before. That's compounding.

Table 4-1. Value of $1 invested today.

Compounding Rate	Years in The Future					
	5	10	15	20	25	30
4%	$1.217	$1.480	$ 1.801	$ 2.191	$ 2.666	$ 3.243
6	1.338	1.791	2.397	3.207	4.292	5.743
8	1.469	2.159	3.172	4.661	6.848	10.063
10	1.611	2.594	4.177	6.728	10.835	17.449
12	1.762	3.106	5.474	9.646	17.000	29.960
14	1.925	3.707	7.138	13.743	26.462	50.950
16	2.100	4.411	9.266	19.461	40.874	85.850
18	2.288	5.234	11.974	27.393	62.669	143.371
20	2.488	6.192	15.407	38.338	95.396	237.376

If you keep at it, your $1.21 will earn 10% during the third year ($0.12), and you'll have $1.33 at the end of the third year; $1.33 + $0.13 = $1.46 at the end of the fourth year; and $1.46 + $0.15 = $1.61 at the end of the fifth. Table 4-1 shows how much $1 invested today would be worth even further into the future at various compounding rates.

If your lucky enough to have $5000 now and you decide to invest it where you can get 6% compounded, you'll have:

5 yrs.	$ 6690	($5000 × 1.338)
10 yrs.	8955	(5000 × 1.791)
20 yrs.	16,035	(5000 × 3.207)

But if you could get a 16% return, your $5000 would grow to:

5 yrs.	$10,500	($5000 × 2.100)
10 yrs.	22,055	(5000 × 4.411)
20 yrs.	97,305	(5000 × 19.461)

And if you're twenty-five or so, endowed with $5000 right now, and smart enough to get 20% compounding per year, that initial $5000 would turn into a cool $7,350,000 by the time you're sixty-five!

Look at the huge differences in the wealth you'd have built in ten, twenty, or thirty years. The differences in those final figures are simply the result of differences in compounding rates. That's why banks or insurance contracts just won't do;

Table 4-2. $1 per year invested at 10% (capital accumulation at the end of each year).

Dollar	Year					
	1	2	3	4	5	6
	Today					
1	$1	$1.10	$1.21	$1.33	$1.46	$1.61
2		1.00	1.10	1.21	1.33	1.46
3			1.00	1.10	1.21	1.33
4				1.00	1.10	1.21
5					1.00	1.10
Total Wealth	$1	$2.10	$3.31	$4.64	$6.10	$6.71

you should not settle for them when you can reasonably expect to do a lot better in the stock market or in real estate.

All that sounds fine. But many of us are faced with a somewhat different problem. We're about $5000 short, and maybe a few years older. If you're starting at zero right now, you've got to make yours out of current income. Different problem, starting at zero—let's say you can set aside $1 each year and you invest it at 10%. Table 4-2 shows what happens to your dollars. Obviously, the first dollar you invested compounds for the full five years, the second for four years, the third for three years, the fourth for only two years, and the last for just one year. Table 4-3 shows you how much $1 invested each year will be worth in the future at various compounding rates. So even if you're at zero net worth today, if you can set aside only $3 a day, and if you can get 12% compounding, in 10 years you'll build a sum of $19,217 ($1095 × 17.55) or $264,256 ($1095 times 241.33) in thirty years.

How big a bundle can you look forward to? Remember, it all depends on how much you've got now, how much you're willing to add to it each year, what rate of return you can earn on it, and how long you've got to build. You can get a good idea of what you can expect by going back to your financial inventory. Take the amount you've got available now for investment from your personal balance sheet. Take the contributions you can add to it each year from your projected income statement. What happens when you compound these amounts

Table 4-3. Value of $1 invested each year (capital accumulation at the end of each year).

Compounding Rate	Years in Future							
	5	*10*	*15*	*20*	*25*	*30*	*35*	*40*
6%	$5.637	$13.181	$23.276	$ 36.786	$ 54.865	$ 79.058	$ 111.435	$ 154.762
8	5.867	14.487	27.152	45.762	73.106	113.283	172.317	259.057
10	6.105	15.937	31.772	57.275	98.347	164.494	271.024	442.593
12	6.353	17.549	37.280	72.052	133.334	241.333	431.663	767.091
14	6.610	19.337	43.842	91.025	181.871	356.787	693.573	1342.025
16	6.877	21.321	51.660	115.380	249.214	530.312	1120.713	2360.757
18	7.152	23.521	60.965	146.628	342.603	790.948	1816.652	4163.213
20	7.442	25.959	72.035	186.688	471.981	1181.882	2948.341	7343.858

over the remainder of your working life at a reasonable compounding rate?

Suppose, for example, that you're in your mid-thirties and you want to retire in your mid-fifties, twenty years from now. You've managed to accumulate $5000, and since your insurance needs are pretty well taken care of and you've got an emergency fund to cover rainy days, you're beginning to think about really making it, or at least retiring in style. You figure that you can contribute $125 a month to your retirement fund and you're willing to learn how to get more than the skimpy bank rate on your investments. Table 4-4 shows what you can expect, given a wide range of compounding rates.

Table 4-4. Value of combined lump sum and annual payments at various compounding rates.

Compounding Rate	Value of $5000 Fund in 20 Years (from Table 4-1)	Value of $1500 per Year in 20 Years (from Table 4-3)	Total Value of Fund in 20 Years
8%	$ 23,305	$ 68,643	$ 91,948
10	33,640	85,913	119,553
12	48,230	108,078	156,308
14	68,715	136,538	205,253
16	97,305	173,070	270,375
18	136,965	219,942	356,907
20	191,690	280,032	471,722

How big is big? It depends on what you need. But I've got to say it again: even the average person can acquire a great deal of wealth if he's willing to set up a plan, if he's willing to sacrifice a little bit today for a great deal tomorrow, and if he has the determination to stick to the program. Carefully consider your own situation—how much you've got now, how much you can add to it, how much you need. Plan your financial future and project your net worth on the well-warranted assumption that you can do better than the bank. In all probability, you can. Rate of return is the critical component, so we've got to do anything that's legal and in our power to get it high and keep it high.

You and Form 1040

Think you work for your own good? Or the company's? Wrong. You work for the government. Out of the half million or more you'll earn in your life, the taxman is going to get at least his fair share. Even if you just plug along at an average income level, the combined federal, state, and local tax take will amount to about one-fifth of your gross earnings. And since you plan to earn a lot more from your career than the average, you can bet that the government's fair share is going to get a lot bigger. And the more you earn, the more wealth and property you've accumulated, the worse it gets.

Let's draw a distinction between your average tax rate and your marginal tax rate, since it's the *marginal bracket* that's most important for your investment decisions. Let's make up some taxable income numbers, compute the average tax rate, and put them into Table 4-5.

Table 4-5. Average and marginal tax rates taken from federal tables for 1977 (assuming joint return with 2 exemptions).

Taxable Income	Taxes Due	Average Tax Rate	Change in Taxable Income	Change in Taxes Due	Marginal Tax Rate
$ 8,000	$ 435	5.4%			
12,000	1,105	9.2	$4,000	$ 670	16.8%
16,000	1,932	12.1	4,000	827	20.7
20,000	2,911	14.6	4,000	979	24.5
24,000	4,011	16.7	4,000	1100	27.5
28,000	5,264	18.8	4,000	1253	31.3

Look, every time you earn an extra thousand, the taxman's take goes up another notch—the faster you make it, the faster they take it! You already knew that the average tax burden increased along with income, but did you realize that the marginal rate is always higher than the average rate? And when you invest to make a buck, it's the marginal rate that applies to those incremental earnings. Even in the middle-income brackets, the government's share of your investment profits can be pretty steep.

How does that affect your investment program? Obviously,

any extra dollars you earn that you have to declare at 1040 time are going to get hit, maybe hit hard. The net effect, of course, is to lower the actual rate of return on your investment capital. Here's an example that should rattle your cage. If you're in the 40% marginal tax bracket, and if you earned 10% on an investment of $10,000—that is, $1000—you'd be left with only $600 after the taxman walked off with his $400 share of your winnings. You'd actually realize only 6% as your after-tax return.

That's the tax-bite situation. To help you determine the potential impact of taxes on your investment returns, Table 4-6 gives the marginal federal tax rate for various levels of income.

Table 4-6. Federal tax rates for 1977.

Taxable Income Single Return	Marginal Tax Rate	Taxable Income Joint Return	Marginal Tax Rate
$12,200–$ 14,200	27%	$ 11,200–$ 15,200	22%
14,200– 16,200	29	15,200– 19,200	25
16,200– 18,200	31	19,200– 23,200	28
18,200– 20,200	34	23,200– 27,200	32
20,200– 22,200	36	27,200– 31,200	36
22,200– 24,200	38	31,200– 35,200	39
24,200– 28,200	40	35,200– 39,200	42
28,200– 34,200	45	39,200– 43,200	45
34,200– 40,200	50	43,200– 47,200	48
40,200– 46,200	55	47,200– 55,200	50
46,200– 52,200	60	55,200– 67,200	53
52,200– 62,200	62	67,200– 79,200	55
62,200– 72,200	64	79,200– 91,200	58
72,200– 82,200	66	91,200– 103,200	60
82,200– 92,200	68	103,200– 123,200	62
92,200– 102,200	69	123,200– 143,200	64
over 102,200	70	143,200– 163,200	66

In addition to the IRS, you're going to get sliced at the state or local levels on your investment earnings as well, and this will increase your total tax burden and lower your effective return even further. You can see that at even relatively modest levels of income, the combination of federal, state, and local taxes is going to take quite a chunk of your investment earnings. That's the bad news.

Now for the good news—the tax laws don't tax all of your investment earnings the same as if you had worked for the money. The money you work for is treated as ordinary income and is subject to full taxation at the marginal rate. But if you invest your money and your investments earn additional money for you, it may be possible to get lower tax rates, or even to defer taxes almost indefinitely—in other words, not pay them at the time you earn the income.

For example, let's suppose you're in the 40% bracket and you do enough overtime work to earn an extra $2000. The taxman will want $800, which leaves you an after-tax net of $1200 for your extra efforts. But if you buy stocks and hold them for two years, receive $100 each year in dividends, and sell them for a profit of $1800 (the same $2000 total income), you'll get to keep more. First, as the tax laws stand now, the $100 dividend will be excluded from your tax-table income in each of the two years. Nice; you don't pay any taxes at all on the first $100 of dividends received in any year ($200 for married couples on a joint return). Next, the $1800 gain will qualify as a long-term capital gain, which is taxed at only half the normal rate. So you'd only pay half the marginal tax rate, or 20% on the gain. (Schedule D makes it appear that you're paying the full marginal rate on half the long-term gain, but the effect is the same.) Thus, out of the $2000 you receive from your investment, the taxman will take only $360 (instead of the $800 he'd gobble up on earned income) and you get to keep the $200 in dividends plus $1440 in after-tax capital gains—a total of $1640 instead of $1200. The same $2000 in extra income, but you keep $440 more if you make it through investment than if you work for it! Think more and work less. There's more money in it for you!

In addition to the partial-dividend exclusion and the favorable long-term capital-gains tax rate, there are a few other bonuses in the tax laws for investors. Say you bet wrong and you had to take a loss on the investment. When you suffer a loss, you can write a part or all of it off against your other income for the year, and thereby reduce your tax bill for that year. That's right. Uncle Sam picks up part of the tab when you lose, just as he takes part of it when you win. Fair enough? That provision—the right to write off a loss against your ordinary income—certainly reduces the net financial consequences of market risk!

But the best parts of the tax laws, as they affect your future wealth, are the two provisions which might give you a way to get immediate *tax exclusions* and *defer taxes* on your investments until you're ready to retire! If you're self-employed, or if you work for someone else but you are not covered by a qualified retirement plan, the tax laws permit you to provide your own fund for retirement. Through two separate programs—the Keogh Plan for self-employed persons, and the Individual Retirement Account (IRA) for those who are not vested in an existing retirement program—you may get a chance to greatly increase your fortune. (If you work for a tax-exempt organization, you may have a similar plan known as Section 403(b)(7) available to you.)

The Keogh Plan, established in 1962, currently allows self-employed persons to invest up to 10% of their income, with a $7500 limit per year, in their own independent retirement fund. The Individual Retirement Account (IRA) was established in 1974. It currently allows persons not covered by a qualified pension plan to invest up to 15% of their income, with a $1500 limit on investments per year ($1750 if a nonworking spouse is included).

Both plans allow you to make investments out of current income, reduce your tax-table income by the amount of the investment, and defer taxes on all investment returns until you retire. Because, in both cases, you can deduct your annual contribution directly from income, it actually costs you less to make an investment. Because you are allowed tax-free accumulation of earnings on your invested capital, your wealth grows faster. And both plans defer taxes until you retire, when, theoretically, you'll either be too infirm to mind being scalped or your tax rate will be lower.

For example, if you qualify for one of the plans and you're in the 40% tax bracket, you can invest $1000 a year in the plan at an after-tax cost of only $600. Since you are reducing your

Table 4-7. After-tax cost of investment in Keogh Plan or Individual Retirement Account.

Amount of Investment	Marginal Tax Rate					
	30%	35%	40%	45%	50%	55%
$ 500	$ 350	$ 325	$ 300	$ 275	$ 250	$ 225
750	525	488	450	413	375	338
1,000	700	650	600	550	500	450
1,250	875	813	750	688	625	563
1,500	1,050	975	900	825	750	675
2,000	1,400	1,300	1,200	1,100	1,000	900
3,000	2,100	1,950	1,800	1,650	1,500	1,350
4,000	2,800	2,600	2,400	2,200	2,000	1,800
5,000	3,500	3,250	3,000	2,750	2,500	2,250

tax-table income by the same amount, you have avoided $400 in taxes which you would ordinarily have given to the tax collector. Table 4-7 makes the cost of investment after taxes a little clearer for various combinations of contribution and tax rate. Notice that the greater your tax bracket, the less it actually costs you to invest under either plan. The point is this: Don't pay the taxman any more than you absolutely, legally have to. Use your money for your own welfare. If you qualify for either of these plans, capitalize on it. Try projecting your income for this year and next, then calculate how much you're currently giving to the IRS, and figure out how little it really costs you to invest.

Let's run through an example to see if we can get a better idea of the advantages these tax-sheltered retirement plans offer us. Again, we'll assume that you're in the 40% marginal tax bracket and that you're willing to put $125 a month (a little over $4 a day) into an IRA plan. Your plan will be maintained by a no-load mutual fund that earns 10% return, compounded annually, over the long term. We'll measure the after-tax advantage of the IRA by comparing it to the same dollar amounts invested in a situation where both the annual contributions and the investment earnings are fully taxable at the marginal rate. Table 4-8 shows the details.

I'm going to assume that you make your contribution to the plan in one lump sum on December 31 of each year. As

Table 4-8. Tax advantage of IRA plan ($1500 per year input, 40% marginal tax rate, 10% annual compounding rate).

Year	---Without IRA---		+++With IRA+++		
	Invested	Wealth Accumulated	After-Tax Cost of Investment	Wealth Accumulated	Tax Advantage
1	$ 1,500	$ 1,500	$ 900	$ 1,500	$ 600
5	7,500	8,456	4,500	9,158	3,702
10	15,000	19,772	9,000	23,906	10,134
15	22,500	34,914	13,500	47,658	21,744
20	30,000	55,179	18,000	85,913	42,734
25	37,500	82,298	22,500	147,521	80,223
30	45,000	118,587	27,000	246,741	146,154
35	52,500	167,153	31,500	406,536	260,383
40	60,000	232,143	36,000	663,890	455,747

you can see in the last column, the first year's tax advantage is simply what you saved in taxes paid by establishing the plan: $600. In every subsequent year, the IRA gives you two separate advantages. First, there's the reduction in your tax tab; you get that just by making the annual contribution. Second, there's the difference in after-tax earnings made possible by the tax deferral provisions of the plan. For example, by year 15 you've saved $9000 ($22,500 – $13,500) in actual taxes simply because you've invested $125 a month in the plan over the years (and have been able to write off your contributions against income). But you've also accumulated more wealth to the tune of $12,744 ($47,658 – $34,914) by virtue of the tax deferral on investment income. So the total advantage of the IRA by year 15 is the sum of *the actual tax savings of $9000* and the *additional wealth accumulated of $12,744* for a final benefit of $21,744. If you're under fifty, the net advantage for your retirement fund of the IRA, or the Keogh if you're self-employed, is colossal!

Since there are a few ifs and buts about who qualifies for each program, it will pay you to check with a tax specialist, preferably a Certified Public Accountant, to see if you qualify. If you plan to set aside money for your retirement, you can't afford to foul up. Pay a few bucks to get the right answer from a qualified person. If you can use either of these tax breaks, you'll find that most no-load mutual funds can offer you both programs. All you have to do to set up your own retirement account is fill out a simple form; your investments will become tax exclusions and the earnings will be tax-deferred. If you can, by all means use the advantage Uncle Sam has given you. It's the only real break the IRS gives us.

A Recap of the Basics

Putting all the pieces in place, you figure you need to shoot for a high return if you're going to beat inflation and build a real stake for your future needs. Since saving accounts, insurances, and that kind of thing give you lots of safety but very little yield, they won't do the job for you. Since you need diversification and marketability for your funds, real estate and mortgages, which are by nature illiquid, are out—unless you've already got a wad and can afford to wait for the right price when you want to sell. The stock market is the only place where you can get the necessary combination of high return and high liquidity. And your best bet there is a no-load mutual fund. You'll get the diversification you need, although you'll still be exposed to the risk of the market. If you qualify, set up a Keogh Plan or an Individual Retirement Account, so you can enjoy its tax advantages. Most of all, stick with your plan for accumulating wealth and, for a while, be satisfied with merely watching your dollars work for you.

I've harped on the idea of using a no-load mutual fund. But I'll bet there's still a thing at the back of your mind about your uncle in Moline. If he were a party to our conversation, he'd surely reckon as how you'd be better off spending your money on a shrink instead of investing it in the stock market. And I'd have a hard time faulting him for his attitude. It's true that a huge number of amateur speculators have been badly burned in mutual funds over the last decade; that's what's helped give the stock market its lousy reputation. Well, where else can we put our money? Maybe we'll just stash it under the mattress. Or—can we find a better place for it? All of which leads to the perfectly logical question, "Just what constitutes a good place for our money as opposed to a not-so-good, or frankly rotten, investment?" So before we get side-tracked by the opportunities in frozen pork bellies or triple-net leasebacks, let's set down a list of attributes we can use to determine what's right for us.

The answer to what's right for us depends on several things. Most importantly, it depends on how old we are now. It also depends on how much money we make now and expect to make in the future; how much we've got stockpiled now; and how interested we are in making more money. I'd bet that we share some similar characteristics, you and I. We're over-worked if not underpaid, we're not overly savvy when it comes to the money-making magic of foreign currencies or numismatics, and we're not already staked with a big bankroll to start our endeavors. At best, we're somewhat ahead of the crowd right now, but we've developed a plan to get way ahead in the future. If that's our starting point, then what's right for us won't be the same as what's right for a high-roller with a stake of $200,000. So we have to ask whether a given invest-ment is suitable for *us,* not for some budding Howard Hughes; and we have to judge on the basis of our present age, income, net worth, education, experience, and motivations.

There are at least five major questions we have to ask in any effort to judge whether an investment is right for us.

1. *How much money can I make?* We already know this as the *expected rate of return.* As we've seen, the average annual com-pounding rate on our investment capital is probably the single most important consideration in our "what's right?" decision. It's obvious that if we can't beat long-term inflation after the taxman has taken his toll, we might as well spend it now! Otherwise, the dollars we'd be investing would actually shrink in terms of their purchasing power over the years. Again, if you were in the 40% tax bracket and if inflation were to con-tinue at 5% per year, you would need to get over 8% per year, just to stay even! The equation:

Percent return − (tax rate × percent return) − inflation rate = net real return

Under that assumption, our absolute minimum requirement for any investment would be an expected long-term, pre-tax return of 8%. Any returns over and above the combination of tax effects and inflation effects obviously work to our advantage by compounding our real wealth. And that, of course, helps move us out of the working class just that much faster.

2. *How much money could I lose?* There are two answers to the question of *risk exposure.* First, there's the chance that you could actually lose part or even all of your investment capital. Second, there's the possibility that you could miss out on a highly profitable play. The risk of actual loss is familiar to most of us: you've bought some stock and its market price goes down. Obviously, you'd have been better off in the bank. The loss of opportunity is just as real a risk, even though it often goes unnoticed. Here's an indication of how important an opportunity missed can be. Suppose you had your money sitting safely in the bank while the stock market was shooting skyward. Your untimely choice of investment has actually cost you money. In other words, your opportunity loss is as real as your actual loss.

Each of these risks has to be traded off against the return you expect to receive. In other words, it would be crazy to take on higher risks unless you expected to get higher returns as a reward. In general, the two go hand in hand. Over the long run, you can expect higher returns if you can afford to bear the higher risks involved.

Fortunately, most of life's risks can be reduced, though not entirely eliminated, by proper planning. As we've said, we can insure against many of life's potentially catastrophic risks. In fact, insurance against catastrophe is a prerequisite for any successful investment program. Investment risks, too, can be made more manageable. For example, diversifying across several different media or several specific situations can almost eliminate the risk of choosing the one that turns sour; even market risk tends to smooth out over longer periods of time. And a long-term perspective—the ability to recognize the speculative cycle in progress—can help to reduce the problem of *when* to buy or sell. Both factors—the chance to achieve diversification, and the ability to adopt a rational view of events as they transpire—are indispensable if we expect to make much money. We'll never hit an instant jackpot using this sane approach, but we should be able to sleep at night, and we can count on being wealthy in the long run.

3. *How much money do I need for openers?* Opening capital requirements play a large part in our choice of an investment vehicle. Initial capital requirements for different kinds of investment media vary considerably, from as little as a few hundred dollars in mutual funds to several thousand dollars for real estate and mortgages. Unfortunately, many of us don't have the several-thousand-dollar chunks it takes to get started in income properties, mortgages, or second-trust deeds and the like. They can be superb investments if you can afford the admission price. But what we're looking for is a play where we can get started on a hundred bucks or less each month, so we'll have to pass the big-ticket window.

4. *How much money do I get to keep?* The *effect of taxation* on our investment earnings, like the size of the initial capital requirement, varies sharply with the different investment media. It's hard to generalize about the tax laws, except to note that they're far too high and far too complex. There are holes, exceptions, exclusions, and preferences that run counter to the law's basic intent. Usually, returns on the more conventional—that is, lower-risk—investments are taxed at ordinary income rates just as if you'd worked for the money, while long-term capital gains are taxed at more favorable— that is, effectively lower—rates. Which only proves what we've already said: it pays to think more and work less. Finally, certain kinds of sheltered investments, which take advantage of specific provisions currently favored in our moralistic tax laws, have become popular in recent years, even though many of them are without economic merit. Watch out for the so-called tax-shelter. We must keep in mind that our primary motive for investment is to make money rather than to obtain a tax advantage. It's usually preferable to pay taxes on our profits than to create an artificial loss that can all too often turn out to be a real loss. Remember that Congress has finally given us the tax break we need in the Keogh Plan and the Individual Retirement Account. Again, a few minutes with an accountant

will help you judge whether you qualify. If you can use either plan, it will help your chances of building a fortune immensely.

5. *How quickly can I get my money if I want it?* The ease with which you can convert your investment assets into hard cash without significantly affecting market price is known as *liquidity*. It's a major concern when you want to change investment strategy. There'll be times when you'll want to get out of a specific asset, and you won't want to wait for weeks or months to do it. Nor will you want to pay a stiff commission, or take a steep discount from prevailing market prices. Some investment media are almost as liquid as cash in the hand; they're the ones with an active and established market, a large number of potential buyers and sellers. In other media, it's all too easy to get stranded without seeing a potential buyer for miles around. Flexibility in our investment strategy is an absolute necessity if we're going to earn really high rates of return without being exposed to excessive risk. Liquidity is therefore extremely desirable.

Obviously, we want to commit our investment capital to media with high expected return, low risk exposure, small capital requirement, favored tax treatment, and instant liquidity. Except—and this may come as a shock to you—situations like that just don't exist. Any investment with all those nice characteristics would appeal to almost everyone, wouldn't it? So everyone, being smart, would switch out of the other media into this swell one. But with all that new capital surging in, its price would go up—and its expected return would go down. And as capital drained out of the less-desirable media, their prices would fall and their expected returns would rise.

Most of the time, the capital markets have ways of balancing out potential risk. This is because money can usually flow easily from one investment medium into another—from one that people perceive as a low return/high risk situation into one they perceive as a high return/low risk opportunity. Notice we said "most of the time." We said, too, that the flow is determined by investors' *perceptions* of risk and return.

If everybody formed their expectations of potential risk and reward on an absolutely rational basis, there'd be very little difference in long-term returns (after proper compensation for varying risk levels) between the various investment media. The fact of the matter, however, is that investors' expectations are based largely on emotional reactions to obvious conditions, with greed and fear as the predominant sensations.

When the mass of investors (or mini-speculators) becomes overly optimistic about the prospects for a particular asset, they stampede in to buy. The stampede can drive prices far above reasonable values, and this is just what happened to stocks in 1968, to gold in 1974, and most recently to real estate. Sooner or later, rationality always conquers, and the natural result is a devastating collapse of market prices. Just as greed can drive prices far above reasonable levels, fear can create bargains for anyone who's more level-headed than the masses. The potential for extraordinary gains is never higher and the risk of actual loss is never lower than when everyone else is scared of, and has been badly burned by, an investment. If you can keep your wits when everyone else is in a panic, you'll make money faster than you can count it. That's not just a wild statement. It's a promise we'll explore as we go along.

The fact remains that there is no one investment that can give us all those ideal characteristics at once. So, at any given time, our job is to search out those that are *good* and are worth buying, and those that are *bad* and ought to be sold *at that moment.* Every form of investment asset has its season, and if we're going to make much money, we're going to have to recognize the changes!

Sure-Fire
Losers

UP to now, we've been talking in general terms about the characteristics of several different investment media. O.K., just to show you how disastrous the most traditional investment vehicles can be to your financial future, let's discuss a couple of the sure-fire losers in a little more detail. People do a lot of crazy things with their money, things they—and we—should avoid. Here are some of the dumbest things you can possibly do with your investment dollars.

Losing Deal #1: Invest Your Money Where It's Safe

Let's start with a conventional savings account, since it's probably the most common investment blunder. From the time you were a little kid, you had the virtue of thrift drummed in your head: if you saved something today, you could buy something better tomorrow. Your dad probably marched you down to the local bank to open your first savings account with the $2.15 you earned doing chores. It was, he lectured, a pad against a rainy day and a start on your personal fortune. It was obviously a good lesson. But it was unintentionally a bum steer as well.

The good lesson, of course, was that you were exposed to the necessity for thrift. But as your first exposure to the world of high finance, it left you with the conception that the bank is a good place for your money. Well, it's not! Yes, it's safe from theft and capital loss, it's liquid, the capital requirement is small, and it's insured. But banks don't pay you enough interest to making saving with them worth the effort. Even in a Time Certificate of Deposit, where you give up liquidity for an extra percent or two, it's nearly impossible to beat the insatiable combination of taxes and inflation over the long haul.

Over the past century, the banks savings rate has ranged from a low of $1^{1}/2\%$ to as high as the recent $5^{1}/4\%$. High, did we say? Look at Chart 5-1. It computes the value of $100 stashed in 1937 in a commercial bank at the prevailing savings rate and contrasts it with the value of $100 invested in the Dow Jones Industrial Average (a measure of the best-grade common stocks), with dividends reinvested over the same forty years. After all that time, you'd have only $372 on deposit in your savings account! That works out to a *pre-tax rate of return* of just under $3^{1}/2\%$ per year compounded annually— then, of course, you would have had to pay income taxes on the interest accrued to your account every year. The interest you earn at the bank is taxable at ordinary income rates in the year in which it's received, while investments in common stocks receive favored tax status. In addition, inflation would have taken another 2% to $2^{1}/2\%$ a year out of the real purchasing power of your savings. So after taxes and inflation you would actually have lost money on the dollars you saved in the bank—to the tune of about 50¢ every year on each $100, assuming you're in the 40% marginal tax bracket. All in all, you'd have almost *six times* as much money if you'd chosen stocks instead of the bank as your investment vehicle!

To figure out how much you'd be losing in a savings ac-

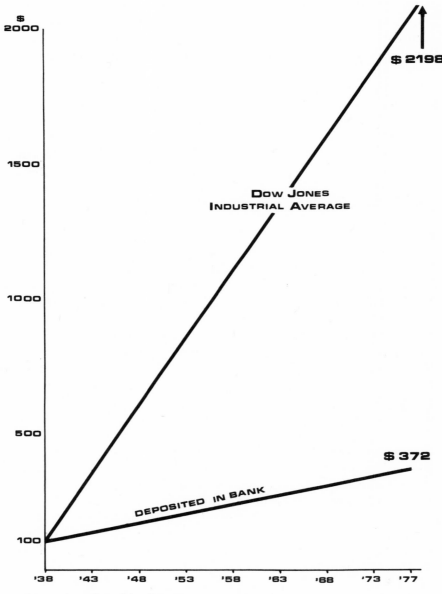

$ 2198

DOW JONES
INDUSTRIAL AVERAGE

$ 372

DEPOSITED IN BANK

'38   '43   '48   '53   '58   '63   '68   '73   '77

Chart 5-1. Value of $100 in 40 years, 1938–1977.

count, simply take the quoted bank rate and multiply that by the figure 1 minus your marginal tax rate. Then subtract the inflation rate. For example, if you've got $1000 in the bank at a 5¹/₄% rate, you earn $52.50 in interest for the year. But assuming you're in a 30% tax bracket, Uncle Sugar is only going to let you keep $36.75 [$52.50 − (.3 × 52.50)] after taxes. If inflation were to run 5% that year, your account would be worth only $987.38 [$1036.75 ÷ 1.05] in real purchasing power. So by playing safe you'd have lost almost thirteen real bucks . . . not a very smooth deal!

The same general commentary applies to Time Certificates of Deposit (TCDs) with just a minor modification. You get an extra point or two of return in a TCD—that is, you don't lose real money quite as fast. But you also give up control over your money in exchange for the higher interest. You have to agree to keep your hands off your money for three or four years, or your earnings revert back to the passbook rate. That means you can't grab a better opportunity if it presents itself. All in all, TCD might be a fair deal if you could count on renewing it at the currently offered 7% to 8% rates when it reaches maturity. There's no promise, however, that the banks will be paying current rates, which are the highest in this century, when renewal time on the current batch of TCDs rolls around. TCDs became hot in the early 1970s when inflation was running in double digits, because bank customers could then choose to *lose less* in a TCD than in a regular savings account. For the banking system, the TCD was a purely defensive reaction; if they hadn't been able to offer the higher rates, depositors would have moved their money out of the banks and savings and loan institutions and into such higher-yield instruments as treasury bills. That chain of events, which is known as disintermediation, could have closed the banks, since they can't operate without your money.

We can reasonably expect the interest rate on TCDs to average 1% to 2% higher than the normal passbook rate. So we have to guess that in future years the long-term rate of return on TCDs will be in the neighborhood of 5% to 5¹/₄% (the historic passbook rate of 3% to 3¹/₂% plus an approximate 2%

premium for the loss of liquidity)—but only *if* the inflation rate returns to its long-term norm of 2% to 2¹/₂%.

That, of course, is the key to monetary rates: the expected rate of inflation in the economic system. All monetary rates include both a *real* return, which is directly related to the risks accepted, and an inflationary premium, which is determined by the expected loss in purchasing power. No one who's at all smart is going to save or loan or invest unless the expected return exceeds the expected loss in purchasing power. So it's more accurate to state probable future returns in relation to some specified inflationary rate. And as we've seen, the real after-tax rate on savings accounts has commonly been negative. TCDs are a slightly better deal than the plain old savings account if you don't mind losing a great deal of flexibility, but they're still not worth writing home about.

All right then. According to our five guidelines for evaluating an investment, cash held—whether under the mattress, in a savings account, in a TCD, in a savings and loan association, or in a credit union—doesn't stack up too well for long-term commitments. Except for TCDs, it's true that liquidity is good, risk factor is minimal, and there are no requirements on the amount you invest. But the low earning rate, the high exposure to inflation, and the unfavorable taxation of interest earned argue against holding cash as an investment. Use your savings account only to build yourself a small emergency reserve fund.

A final note. There are special exceptions to all this, such as advanced age when we can't risk capital, or when we see indications of an impending top in a speculative cycle and we know that the risk of loss outweighs the potential for gain. These situations may dictate a completely liquid position now and then, and we'll go into that later. But your investment dollars do not belong in the bank for any extended time period.

Losing Deal #2: Invest and Protect at the Same Time

One of the big insurance companies promises "financial independence through a planned program of insurances."

They've got a better chance of floating the Titanic! Most insurance contracts are atrocious when it comes to helping you invest for your future.

I've said it before and I'll say it again. Insurance has one basic purpose: to provide financial protection against the consequences of certain catastrophic events. In its proper place a reasonable amount of insurance is absolutely essential. But beyond the necessary protection, insurance contracts are a waste of your investment dollars. In most forms of insurance, the premiums you pay are divided between the costs of basic protection, the ante for sales commissions (which could run to a substantial percentage of your total payments over the life of the contract), and a share of the insurance company's operating costs and profits. To the extent that you're buying financial protection you can't provide for yourself, you get what you pay for. But some types of insurance programs (most notably whole-life, endowment, and annuity contracts) contain investment elements as well as protection—and it's in the investment area that insurance programs fall flat on their faces.

Let's take a typical contract for whole-life insurance. You have contracted to pay a larger premium than you would on a straight-term basis for the identical protection. A considerable slice of your premium dollar goes to the guy who sold you the contract. After further deductions for protection, company costs, and profits, some portion of that higher premium (the portion usually increases as you get older) goes into a savings program. There it earns interest at the rate specified in the insurance contract—a rate that is usually guaranteed, but is unfortunately low. Since you're forced to save—you've got to make the premium payments—there's a high probability that you'll accumulate something over the years. That something is called the cash surrender value, and you can borrow against it, or obtain it outright by cancelling the contract. Obviously, you do have decent liquidity on a relatively safe investment. The catch, and it's a big one, is that you usually earn less on the non-insurance portion of your premium than you would at a bank or savings and loan or credit union. So unless the only way you can force yourself to invest in your future is by having a contractual commitment to pay the premium, you'd be better off buying the lowest-cost protection that fits your needs. Then you can use the difference in premium payments to invest on your own *and* at much higher rates of return.

The same defects that plague whole-life insurance contracts—extremely poor rates of return and commission loads—also characterize most of the endowment and annuity contracts currently offered by major underwriters. The endowment type of policy is usually purchased with a specific objective in mind—education, retirement, or some other special foreseeable need. It provides both protection during the life of the contract and cash surrender, at the face value of the contract at maturity. Since endowment contracts are primarily savings plans, the premiums are usually higher than on either term or whole-life. If you can depend on yourself to invest, if you don't need the pressure of a contract to make you save, you can probably do considerably better than the paltry rate you can expect on most endowment contracts.

Annuities, however, do have their place in your investment program, even though their earning rates are generally low. As you near retirement, and you can no longer afford to take market risks with all your funds, some of your accumulated wealth could be used to purchase a straight life annuity. This would guarantee a minimum income level for the remainder of your days. Of course, it would be a terrible deal if you passed away only a year or two after you bought it; the insurance company would have beat the actuarial odds in that case. But if you lived to see a hundred (the underwriter is betting that you'll make seventy-five or eighty at the outside), you'd get those payments for thirty or forty years. In other words it could be an extremely good investment if you expect to hang around for a long time. Again, you have potential inflation to consider anytime you buy a fixed-dollar annuity. So even at advanced age, only a small part of your assets should go into an annuity. Despite the inexhaustible stream of income, the earning rates are too low to warrant investment of a major portion of your capital.

On balance, insurances suffer from two glaring faults: an

inferior return on invested capital, and commission load charges. Insurances, of course, do what they're supposed to do very well. They provide financial security against the risk of living (disability, property loss, personal liability, health care, extended unemployment, and continuing income in your later years) as well as income for your beneficiary if you die. The forced-saving feature of the life programs is something of a plus. But for the vast majority of your investment assets, you can earn somewhat higher returns at the same level of risk or much better returns with a moderate increase in risk. If you can muster the discipline to take the one step I've been urging all along—pay yourself first every month—there are much better places for your investment dollars than insurance.

Losing Deal #3: Lend Your Money to Someone

Not to just anyone. Lend your money only to someone who's creditworthy. And charge them interest on the loan. After all, that's how the banks and the savings and loans make their money, isn't it? They use their depositors' money, for which they pay 5% or 6%, to make loans at higher rates, and they get rich on the spread. Why shouldn't you do the same thing?

There are quite a few reasons.

First, you're not a bank or savings and loan, so you don't have the facilities to find out who's creditworthy and who's not. You might be able to overcome that defect by having your prospective borrower pledge some property to guarantee re-payment. Or you might decide to restrict your loans only to those borrowers whose creditworthiness you can determine from outside sources. But how practical is that?

Second, have you ever heard of usury statutes? Lots of states have laws that specify the maximum rate of interest you can legally charge for a loan. The problem is that many of those laws were put on the books a long time ago, when interest rates were generally much lower than they are now. So in many states it's illegal for you to earn more than 10% or so by

lending your money, no matter how good or bad the borrower's credit rating may be. "Hey," you say, "that can't be
true. My plastic money costs me 18% a year if I don't pay up
every month. How come my bank gets 18% if it's not legal?"
Cute trick: in many states, the established financial institutions
are exempted from the usury laws. So it's perfectly O.K. for
them to shark; the laws only prevent you and me from getting
in on the action.

Finally, how are you going to get your money back if the
borrower doesn't repay you as he promised? Sue the bastard?
Foreclose on the mortgage? That should take anywhere from
six months to five years and it could cost you thousands in
legal fees. At that, even if you were successful, you'd have
been deprived of the income you could have earned. All the
while, you'll be involved in a real battle to get the property
that was pledged as collateral—and it's not likely to be in A-1
condition if and when it's eventually turned over to you. The
only answer to the default problem is to make sure that one or
two bad loans won't completely smash your net worth. And
the only way to do that is to ensure that no single loan makes
up more than a very small percentage of your total portfolio.

The only good loan portfolio is one that is well diversified,
with lots of small loans to lots of different borrowers. Banks
diversify their loan portfolios; savings and loans diversify; finance companies diversify; even pawnbrokers diversify. If
you're crazy enough to try to compete with them, knowing
that you're the one facing the usury laws, knowing that you
don't have access to the credit information they do, diversification is the only way you can get any protection.

"Well, how am I going to get diversified on $100 a
month?" you ask. Individually, you aren't! The huge initial
capital requirement puts the mortgage market completely out
of reach to people like you and me. Mortgages secured by real
property generally start at around $10,000 and run up from
there, although you might be able to find a few second
mortgages in the $3000 to $5000 range. The rates on
mortgages are usually a point or two higher than on quality
corporate bonds, but they can vary considerably depending on

such factors as the credit rating of the borrower, the collateral pledged, and changing money market conditions. Then, if you were to invest in a mortgage on your own, your capital would be tied up for between five and thirty years. If you needed it for any reason, you'd have to discount the mortgage by 30% or more—that is, sell it for less than its face value—just to get your money out. Large initial capital requirement, extreme illiquidity, and an absolute necessity for broad diversification—no wonder the commercial loan and mortgage markets are almost completely dominated by the banks and S&Ls.

The point is that you'd need at least $50,000 to $100,000 just to start building a decent portfolio of first and/or second mortgages. And you'd have to be willing to commit your capital for a long period of time. There's a place for mortgages and seconds once you've accumulated a very large amount of capital. They give reasonably good rates of return and are reasonably safe when the portfolio is well diversified, so they can be excellent vehicles for wealth preservation. They can be especially useful in later years. But mortgages are too big-league when you're starting from scratch.

Losing Deal #4: The Bond Market

"O.K., how about giving up a point or two and opting for the bond market?" Well, lets look at that alternative. A bond, like a mortgage, is just a loan you're making to a borrower—this time to a government or corporate borrower. One of the primary differences between the two is that while virtually all mortgages are secured by something physical, some piece of real property, bonds may or may not be secured by anything tangible. So while you may be able to foreclose on some deadbeat whose mortgage you're holding, or take legal claim to a house after an extended hassle, it's even more difficult to get your money when some government entity or defunct business concern is in default on one of its bonds. It's true that some corporate bonds are secured by physical property; useful stuff like railroad cars and steam-boilers are popular for the purpose, since you're not likely to get much satisfaction out of recovering your share of a car-coupling unit. But the vast majority of bonds outstanding today are completely dependent on the continued earning power or revenue-generating capability of the issuer.

When you buy a bond, you get promoted to the status of a first-class creditor. You are the holder of a senior security. If that sounds impressive, it only means that the borrower will try to pay *you* before he pays the stockholders, and if he can't pay, you'll get first crack at the corporate corpse. In other words, your bond is an I.O.U. from the issuer. He guarantees to pay you a fixed number of dollars each year in interest—if he can. He also guarantees to pay you back your $1000 of principal when the bond matures—if he can. If he can, everything's fine; but if he can't, you've got problems. Let's look at the problems.

The biggest issuer of bonds in the world is us—U.S.—Uncle Sam—the federal government. Uncle Sam issues bonds, notes, and bills in all denominations from $1000 up. If he couldn't pay them off (remember, he's the guy who collects the taxes and prints the money) then we'd all have problems. But with all the resources available to him through taxation or confiscation, what are the chances that Uncle Sam won't be able to pay his bills? None. There's virtually no risk of default on the short-term government obligations known as treasury bills, so they sell at yields that set the floor for all other interest rates.

Except under unusually tight monetary conditions, the risk-free treasury bill will be the lowest-yield debt security around. All other securities will be tied to it at interest rates that rise in proportion to the level of risk, as you see in Chart 5-2. Even the best corporations, those with Aaa ratings, can run across tough times with the chance that they won't be able to make the required interest and principal payments. As the risk of financial loss increases—from governments to high-grade corporates to lower-grade corporates to defaulted bonds—yields generally rise to compensate for the higher risk. In addition, yields normally increase as the time to maturity of

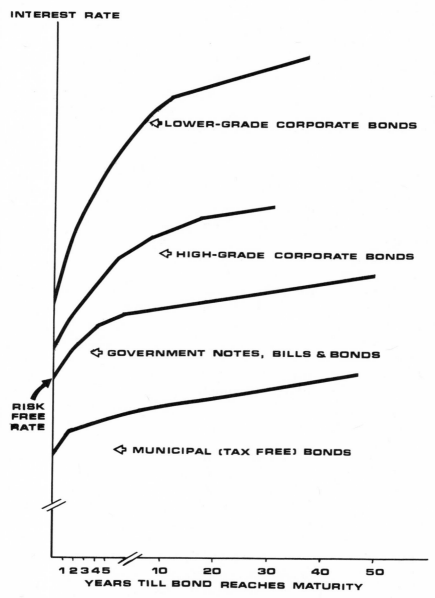

INTEREST RATE

⟨⊢ LOWER-GRADE CORPORATE BONDS

⟨⊢ HIGH-GRADE CORPORATE BONDS

⟨⊢ GOVERNMENT NOTES, BILLS & BONDS

RISK
FREE
RATE

⟨⊢ MUNICIPAL (TAX FREE) BONDS

1 2 3 4 5   10   20   30   40   50
YEARS TILL BOND REACHES MATURITY

Chart 5-2. Yield curve and yield spreads.

the bond increases, on the principle that the distant future is riskier and more uncertain than the near future. Again, the higher the risk, the higher the return. Of course, municipal bonds, those issued by state and local governments, have the lowest yield because they're not taxed by the federal government.

As a general rule, the yield on bonds with about five years or more to maturity reflects what investors think the long-term inflation rate will be, plus a small real return tacked on to compensate for the financial risk borne by the bondholder. Since both the interest and the principal to be paid at maturity are specified in the bond contract as a fixed number of dollars, any change in bond yields has to be made by changing the market price of the bond! Take a look at Table 5-1, and see what happens, as the interest rate changes, to the price of a bond that guarantees to pay $50 per year forever.

To simplify our example, we assume we will never get our $1000 principal back; with most bonds, of course, we would. Fortunately, several financial services provide yield-to-maturity (YTM) data which include the amortization of any discount (paid if the bond was bought below its par value) or premium, so we're spared the trouble of calculating these figures ourselves.

There are two important points to be taken from Table 5-1. First, even though tradition considers them safe since they're senior securities, *bonds are risky* investments, since changes in the market rate of interest can cause dramatic changes in their prices. Second, bonds can be extremely profitable investments when long-term interest rates are falling! As we've found out, long-term interest rates are determined largely by other investors' inflationary expectations. If the future brings less inflation than those investors expect, bonds could be extremely profitable holdings. And since bonds, mortgages, and common stocks all compete for the same investment dollars, lower levels of inflation would certainly be a positive influence on all three markets.

Before we can generalize about expected returns from bonds, we'll have to specify the inflation rate we expect to see in the future. Right now, looking into the 1980s and beyond,

Table 5-1. Interest rates and bond prices.

Market Interest Rate	Price of Bond	Interest/Market Value = Current Yield	Change in Bond Price
9%	$ 556	$50/556 = 0.09	
			$ 69
8	625	50/625 = 0.08	
			89
7	714	50/714 = 0.07	
			119
6	833	50/833 = 0.06	
			167
5	1,000	50/1,000 = 0.05	
			250
4	1,250	50/1,250 = 0.04	
			417
3	1,667	50/1,667 = 0.03	
			833
2	2,500	50/2,500 = 0.02	

it's hard to imagine anything less than a continuing inflation rate of 5% to 6% or even more. History indicates, however, that sustained steady inflations are the exception rather than the rule. Usually inflation turns rampant or it busts. In the American experience, three other major inflationary periods, each coinciding with the end of an important war (1814, 1864, and 1920), were all followed by an unexpected return to price stability or deflation. Perhaps the current case will prove to be the exception. But if inflation drops back to its long-term norm of 2% to $2^{1}/_{2}$%, then nominal bond yields could drop to 4% to 5%—with a capital gain (doubling) for the bond buyer who buys at the currently available 8% to 10%. If that were to happen in, say, the next fifteen or twenty years, it would work out to a 3% to 4% annual rate of capital gain in addition to the 8% to 10% current yield: a total return of around 11% to 14% per year compounded. That's not necessarily a prediction. It's just an indication of how important unanticipated changes in inflation rates are to the bond market.

Nevertheless, I should mention that bonds haven't done too well in the last fifty years—in itself a strong reason to suspect that they won't in the next fifty. During the fifty-year period from 1926 to 1975, bonds averaged less than a 4% total return when both interest received and capital changes were taken into account. Actually, we can get a lot more detailed than that, since the rates of return for both bond investments and common stock investments have been carefully recorded and analyzed over long periods of time. We're thus in a position to know what to expect on the basis of those hard numbers from the past. The inferences we can make from past stock and bond returns provide us with very reliable guides to future expectations—an added bonus in our long-term planning.

Let's take a look at the long fifty years between 1926 and 1975. Practically anything that can happen to a country, short of revolution or annihilation, happened to America during that half century. We lived through victorious wars, tragic wars, booms, depressions, recessions, recoveries, assassinations, riots, flying saucers, and atomic bombs, all of it just about par for the course in developed countries. We can't expect things to be too different in the next fifty years, which means we can reasonably look for similar investment results in the future. In any case, these statistics provide the best estimate we've got.

In Table 5-2, we've summarized the annualized rate of return for corporate bonds including interest and capital changes for one-year, five-year, and ten-year periods over that fifty-year slice of history.

Now I confess that I'm inclined to concentrate on the betting odds for any investment, so let me explain what Table 5-2 might mean to a bookmaker. Actual losses occurred in ten of the fifty one-year periods, when bond prices fell as interest

Table 5-2. Corporate bonds: total returns for 1926–1975 (percent per year compounded).

	1-Year Periods	5-Year Periods	10-Year Periods
1/6 of returns over	9.2%	6.2%	5.3%
Average return	3.8	3.7	3.4
1/6 of returns under	−1.5	1.1	1.5
Percent showing profit	80	96	100

rates rose. In other words, the betting odds for making *some* money in the bond market in any single year were about 4:1 in your favor. And yet, over those fifty years, the total return on corporate bonds averaged only very slightly more than the banks savings rate—not very impressive when you consider the risks investors took by holding bonds. From Table 5-2, we have to conclude that bond returns have usually been quite low, although there has been some variation in returns depending on the level of, and the direction of change in, interest rates. It's the constant shifting of those interest rates that causes bond prices to fluctuate, and that's why we've included high returns and low returns in the table.

About two-thirds of all bond transactions fall between the high and low extremes, and that spread is a measure of how risky the asset has been and therefore how risky it's likely to be in the future. In terms of the betting odds, it's about 5:1 in your favor that you would do at least as well as the row marked "1/6 of returns under"; conversely, it's about 5:1 against your making any more than the row labeled "1/6 of returns over." So if you're looking for 20% per year in the bond market, you can see that it's possible, but it's certainly not very probable. In other words, you're bucking the odds. You can also see that the spread between high returns and low returns decreases rapidly as the holding period increases from one year to five, and again as it increases from five years to ten. That's important. It means that your chance of actually losing money, as well as your chance of making a killing, decreases constantly the longer you play the game. In other words, the few extremely good years make up for the few bad years and your long-term results will close in on the average! So if you were to undertake a bond investment program at some point in the future and if you decided to hold those bonds for ten years, your best guess of the earning rate would be about 3.4%; and your best guess for the bank savings rate would be 3.3%. By comparing the two, you could see that bonds have a slightly higher expected earning rate than savings accounts, but they also face the possibility of loss.

The ability to make comparisons between two potentially attractive investments is extremely useful; in fact, it's the only way you can make a rational choice. That's why the availability of past risk/return data for most of the financial markets is an important factor in deciding where to put your money—it tells you what to expect, always assuming that the future's something like the past. And our operating assumption is that the next fifty years will be similar in structure to the last fifty.

Just as important as the estimate they give of future returns is the clear picture of the risk/return trade-off these numbers provide. In other words, on the basis of past information, you can draw conclusions about the relative attractiveness of various investments. For example, Table 5-3 lists fifty-year rates of return for four of the most popular investment instruments and it allows you to draw some generalizations that should hold in the future. There's a terribly important message in that table: *low risk = low return; high risk = high return!*

Table 5-3. Comparative risk/return relationships for fifty one-year periods from 1926–1975.

	Risk-Free (Treasury Bills)	Very Low Risk (Savings)	Low Risk (Corporate Bonds)	High Risk (NYSE Stocks)
$1/6$ of returns over (%)	4.5%	4.6%	9.2%	44.3%
Average return	2.3	3.3	3.8	13.3*
$1/6$ of returns under (%)	0.2	2.1	−1.5	−17.7
Percent showing profit	100	99+	80	60

*Tax advantages and leverage may increase these returns.

Now you know the odds. You can see that the average rate on treasury bills closely parallels the 2.3% long-term inflation rate. The result is that an investor in the 30% marginal tax bracket would end up losing real purchasing power at a rate of 0.7% per year. That is, $2.3 - (.3 \times 2.3) - 2.3 = -0.7$ or earning rate − (tax rate × earning rate) − inflation rate = real after-tax earning rate. "Well, if that's the case, why would anyone use treasury bills?" Two reasons. First, because the money is perfectly safe. Second, because treasury bills are used only for short-term investments, and it's better to earn something than nothing, even if they do lose to inflation slightly. In other words, it's better to lose 0.7% per year than 2.3% per year. For long-term investments, though, treasury bills are out.

The numbers also show that you're not doing too well in the banks either. Figure it out: $3.3 - (.3 \times 3.3) - 2.3 = 0.0$. You're breaking even after taxes and inflation. Banks rely on safety, liquidity, and ingrained tradition to attract depositors but they're lousy places for your investment capital. Insurances and (as we've seen) high-grade bonds don't average much more than the inflation rate, so obviously they aren't going to be much help to your wealth-building program. You *need earning power, not just safety!*

"Now wait a minute," you're saying, "I can go out right now and get 5% on my savings, or 7% to 8% in a Time Certificate of Deposit, or maybe 8% to 9% in high-grade corporate bonds, and even 9% to 10% in mortgages. So why do you keep telling me they only pay 2% to 4%?" Well, you're right. As it stands today, you *can* get 5% to 10% *nominal* yields in relatively safe media. But remember what we've been talking about. Are they providing *real* returns after inflation and taxes? In the long run, *real return is directly related to the risks you've accepted*. Take a look at Table 5-4.

The inescapable lesson of the last fifty years is that you get paid, and paid well, for accepting risk. Let's qualify that one

Table 5-4. Pre-tax real (after-inflation) returns and risk for forty-six five-year periods from 1926–1975.

	Risk Accepted				
	None (Treasury bills)	Low (Savings)	Moderate (Bonds)	High (Real Estate 1959–1977)	High (Stocks)
Nominal one-year return	2.3	3.3	3.7	7.7*	10.7*
Less inflation	−2.3	−2.3	−2.3	−2.3	−2.3
Before-tax real return	0.0	1.0	1.4	5.4*	8.4*

*Tax advantages and leverage may increase these returns.

iota. *You get paid for taking risks—like market risks—that cannot be avoided. You don't, repeat don't, get paid for taking risks that are not necessary.* Otherwise pony players and crapshooters would be at the upper end of the economic order.

Over and over again, we come back to the same conclusion. If you're really serious about making money on your investments, you'll have to be willing to accept the higher risks associated with real estate and common stocks. Keep in mind that both offer significant tax advantages over the fixed-income investments, and that increases their potential after-tax return. And both allow you to use leverage—that is, other people's money, borrowed from savers to finance your holdings—to magnify your gains. Of course, you also magnify your losses if you hit the market wrong!

So let's forget about long-term investments anywhere other than in real estate or in the stock market.

Two Potential Winners

ALL right then. It's real estate or stocks—both, if you can swing it. It won't be easy, but it's much more likely that you can learn how to operate successfully in these areas than almost any other investment area. That's because both markets have well-defined guidelines that can shift the odds of winning considerably in your favor, and because both markets have strongly rising long-term trend values. As we all know, a great many fortunes have been made in real estate. Small speculators and well-financed corporate operators alike understand the financial implications of the broker's favorite phrase, "Always more people but no more land."

Let's look at the investment merits of real estate. We'll find at least three different motives for owning it. First, there's home ownership. Second, there's real estate held for income production. And third, there's real estate held as a speculative investment. Each of these three forms of ownership has a very different appeal to potential investors: let's briefly review them.

Owning one's own home is part of our heritage. It's so deeply ingrained in our traditions that nearly two-thirds of all American families own or are buying their homes. Renting, as opposed to buying, is the economic equivalent of masochism in our society. You lose the psychic income, your credit rating suffers, and you don't get any tax advantages. Home ownership gives you a certain security and status in your community, it does wonders for your ability to borrow, and it can reduce your taxable income by the amount of your interest and property-tax payments. For families everywhere, owning the roof over their heads has been an excellent investment over the years. For many, the equity they've built in their house, as they've had to make monthly mortgage payments over the years, is the only way they've been able to accumulate anything.

It's extremely difficult to put hard numbers on returns from home ownership. There are too many variables in the equation—such as original purchase price, hidden expenses, mortgage terms and interest rate, size of the down payment, location and demographic changes in the area (which affect the rate of appreciation or depreciation), and tax advantages. And there aren't enough historical data available on which to base measures of past returns.

All this lack of hard data makes guesstimating future returns from any kind of real estate venture subject to larger-than-normal forecasting errors. With that disclaimer in mind, we'll make that guess: it's probably reasonable to expect a return of 7% to 8% per year on a wisely-bought personal residence using long-term history as our guide.

"Hey, that's way too low, isn't it? I know a guy who bought a new house and made $10,000 on it before it even cleared escrow—that's a hell of a lot more than 7% or 8%." I know that the 7% to 8% range sounds too low, especially since prices have nearly doubled in this decade. (They've gone from $28,900 in 1970 to $53,100 in 1977 for the average new house, an increase of about $9\frac{1}{2}$% per year compounded.) Nevertheless, on the average, 7% to 8% seems to be a realistic expectation on a typical house bought for 100 times its monthly rental value. That, if you recall, is the old banker's rule designed to keep you from jumping in near the top of a roaring land boom. Remember our $300 rental back in Chapter 3? Based on that rule, you'd be fairly safe in buying the house for something in the range of $24,000 to $36,000. When the same $300-a-month house lists on the market for $45,000 or more, when there's lots of front-page news about the "housing shortage," when the brokers are hawking their "no more land" slogan, and when people queue up for a "last chance to buy before prices go out of sight," it's getting late in the speculative cycle and even home ownership may not be a good place for your money.

An increasing segment of our population believes that "prices *have* to go up or, at worst, level off." Remember the nature of speculative demand? For us as investors, there's a critical difference between what we have called functional (or useful) demand on the one hand and speculative demand on the other. When we talked about speculative demand in reference to the stock market, we found that it was the primary cause of cycles in stock prices. Let's give it a rerun, since it works almost exactly the same way in real estate. Again, the same line of reasoning applies to most other investment media, from bonds to common stocks to gold to art and so on. Almost any asset that isn't immediately consumed, and on which the price is determined by buyers and sellers in an auction environment, can be subject to bouts of speculation from time to time. And it's the emotional makeup of us little guys that allows speculation to get started in the first place: our tendency to reach fever pitch on the way up, and dive into sheer panic in the terminal throes of the crash that inevitably follows.

We'll use the example we used before to illustrate the distinction between functional demand and speculative demand in real estate. What was the motive behind that house you bought for $30,000 after you'd taken the trouble to check out comparable rentals in the area at $300 a month? That was functional demand at work. O.K., you've now got this nice home in a small, quiet town in the southwest where nothing special happens. One evening network news comes on with a story about the severe winter in the east, and the consequent migration into the sunbelt. Well and good—a news item in proper proportion—there is certainly *some* net migration into the sunbelt.

But where there are vivid imaginations at work, facts sometimes are blown way out of proportion. So when you hear the story from the local tavernmaster a few days later, his account has the combined populations of New York and New Jersey moving into your town within a couple of years. Acting on the rumor, some of the "smarter" townspeople have already begun buying up all the property that's available, since those new people are going to need somewhere to live, right? Speculative demand has entered the market, and is beginning to affect prices.

Now, if people were really rational, they would stop at this point and check out a few of the facts in the fable's development. And that would be the end of the "boom." But such mundane, common-sense questions as "Where are all those people going to find work?" would only spoil the party, so nobody bothers to ask. A few hot tips exchanged over beers and back fences, and the story's on its way, blown out of all proportion.

The cycle has begun. Housing prices have probably edged up a step because a few early speculators and real estate brokers have bought up the existing supply. This initial price rise creates an incredible chain of events. People *want* to believe the rumor, and they pounce on that first price rise as confirmation of its validity. Prices are now expected to rise even more because they have been rising recently ... the trend psychology at work. From this point on, it is imperative that each successive price rise be followed by the release of some good news, at least a portion of which will be manufactured in greedy imaginations, in order to justify the preceding rise, and to provide more fuel to stoke the speculative fires.

With the mass migration to the sunbelt willingly accepted as gospel, and with brokers hawking their "more people, no more land" theme, interest in real estate grows among the locals. Accordingly, it becomes fashionable to be a real estate investor, since that is regarded as a visible symbol of financial sophistication, and housing prices begin moving up. Reflecting the newly found prosperity, owners sell their homes and use the profits to buy bigger and fancier homes. Or they refinance their present homes and use the proceeds to make new down payments on expanded holdings. As the upward progression gains speed, new speculators come in from the outside, attracted by the rising prices. Usually, these late buyers have to be willing to await their hoped-for profits from "expected price appreciation" in order to justify prices, which have escalated far beyond historic values. Of course, as everyone will tell you, things are different this time around, so the old rules don't apply anymore. "If you can count on 10% to 15% a year in appreciation, what does it matter if you're paying 150 times the monthly rental for it? You'll make your money in capital gains. After all, there aren't enough houses here for all those new people, so prices *have* to keep going up!"

Speculative demand feeds on its past success: an unbroken string of price increases convinces all except the very skeptical (in this case, the very smart) that prices will *always* go up. But the price increases have set two forces in motion, irrevocable forces that will eventually and inevitably break the bubble. First, the higher prices have set off a new wave of home-building, adding a new supply of housing to a market where the demand is largely speculative. Second, since houses now cost so much, a growing portion of the local citizenry has been priced out of the market. In other words, it will take outsiders with new money to keep the momentum going.

Now we've got a situation where the supply is increasing on the one hand and the potential demand for *functional usage* is decreasing on the other. If prices are to keep going up, either the supply has to be relatively restricted, or the potential demand has to come increasingly from outside speculators. So we have all the characteristics of the speculative market at its top: growing supply as a natural consequence of past price increases, waning potential demand as the functional users are priced out of the market, and increasing dependence on new money from new speculators to sustain higher price levels. At this point, prices can still go up, but the odds are fading fast.

It's been some time since network's factual commentary

triggered off this stampede. Since you've made a bundle on paper and you can see that the rate of increase is slowing, you decide, wisely, that it's time to lock in some of those gains. There's no way you could know it, but you put your house on the market the day after it reaches the final top. You just watched your neighbor bail out at $60,000, and you feel that's enough. So you make your move at the same price the very next day . . . but no takers. You wait a couple of weeks, and then you decide to accept an offer at $58,000. And in the process you make a bunch of other speculators very, very nervous! They've been watching the market too, and they get worried when they see a down-tick in prices. Remember, they've been holding on in anticipation that prices will continue to go up. Once they see selling prices move down, they figure they'll have to reconsider their thinking!

The fast, the smart, the experienced speculator doesn't wait too long to decide. If things don't go as he expected, he gets out! In quick succession, the wiser speculators now begin putting their properties on the market, even accepting somewhat reduced prices to ensure quick sales. "Just a correction, not a trend! Nothing to worry about," counsels the broker who's now the most respected financial genius in town. "Hey, you interested in a cute little two-bedroom unit over on Fourth? After all, one thing is sure—they're not making any more land!"

But when the smart speculators stepped out, they left that telltale track: lower prices. Now the second round of speculators is worried. Maybe this ride has gone a little far; maybe it's time they got out too. So they add a new batch of houses to the market, and they accept offers at even lower prices. Rounds three and four are pretty much the same, as rank after rank of speculators lets go at reduced prices. Then, after several more additions to supply and several new rounds of falling prices, someone finally decides to check the facts. Yes, it was cold in New England last winter. And yes, there is a net migration out of the northeast and into the sunbelt. However, at current rates, it would take twenty years to move a population the size of Buffalo into your state. And very few of them would end up in your town, since it's obvious there are no jobs there.

The facts are out, just as they should have been before this little boom got underway. All those houses up for sale aren't really needed. And it isn't over yet. There are still a few speculators left who are forced to sell at almost any price because they can't keep up the mortgage payments on empty houses. Near the end, there will be a glut on the market, but nobody will be interested anymore.

Exaggerated? Yes! Implausible? No. The speculative cycle—propelled by dreams of riches without effort on the upside and by utter confusion on the drop—is characteristic of almost every investment market where there are potential buyers and prospective sellers. Our one advantage is that we may be able to recognize the cycle for what it is. If we can separate price from value in our minds, we might come close to being sellers near the cycle's top and buyers near the bottom! That arrangement will help us make a lot of money.

The whole purpose of the sunbelt example was to illustrate again the important distinction between functional demand and speculative demand. It's the functional demand for any asset—its use in fulfilling people's needs for food, shelter, and materials, its use in the production and distribution system, and its use in generating income—that determines its *intrinsic value*. But the price of almost any investment asset can be driven considerably above its intrinsic value on waves of speculative enthusiasm. And it can be driven well below its true value when sellers panic and buyers can't be found. Speculative demand operates more subtly in the real estate market than in the stock market simply because the price changes in real estate are not as widely monitored by small investors. But the speculative element is always present. And since we're contemplating real estate for our investment dollars, we've got to be aware of it.

As an investment medium, real estate offers just about every combination of risk and return, from low-risk income-producing units to high-risk raw land speculation. Though data on real estate risk and return are rather hard to come by,

Table 6-1. Some typical real estate returns.

Item	Period	Percent per Year Compounded
Average farmland per acre	1960–1975	8.8%
Average farmland per acre	1967–1977	10.5
Residential lot (average)	1967–1977	6.3
New home (median)	1967–1977	5.4
New home (median)	1970–1977	9.9
Value of all real estate	1959–1969	6.1
Value of all real estate	1967–1977	9.8
Value of all real estate	1959–1977	7.7

and the returns vary greatly, we can get an idea of the historic results from Table 6-1. As a general rule, the typical investment in income-producing property has produced yields that are competitive with those on common stocks after the tax advantages have been considered. In addition, it's possible to use greater amounts of leverage, that is, borrowed money, in real estate than in almost any other investment medium. Leverage, of course, is a terrific advantage when prices are rising, but it can really hurt when they're falling.

Good yields, high leverage, and tax breaks are appealing aspects of real estate investment, but the medium has some limitations as well. Real estate investments are noted for their poor liquidity; obviously, they can't be converted to cash very quickly. Many require a considerable degree of managerial effort and expertise on the owner's part. With historical data so meager, there's also the problem of trying to figure out what has happened in the past, so we can predict what will happen in the future. For our purposes, however, real estate has one insurmountable shortcoming. And that is the large amount of capital required to get into the game. Our few hundred dollars a year (or the couple of thousand bucks we might have now) just won't go very far toward building a diversified portfolio of income-producing property or raw land. Therefore, until we're several years into the investment process, our need for diversification effectively eliminates real estate as an investment media. Once you've accumulated the first twenty thousand dollars or so, spreading out to include real estate could be a smart maneuver. But that's an entirely different ballpark than the one we're playing in now!

If I haven't convinced you before, I think you'll have to agree now. The stock market is the only game in town—at least until we've accumulated a pretty fair-size stack of chips. So let's learn the ground rules of the only game that's available to us. Some of this material we've touched on before, but it's vital. So bear with me. It's your fortune, remember!

"The Dow Jones Industrial Average was down another eight points today," reports the same announcer who brings you all the other good news—wars, politics, sports, weather. Twenty-five million investors own shares in American enterprise, and that eight-point drop represents capital that just vanished into thin air. Sure, stocks are risky! You can lose real money out there. *But you can make money out there too!* I'll concede that more folks have lost money than have made it, but those few who have made it have made a bundle! And armed with a plan, you can too!

"Well if it's so damned easy, why have twenty million of those suckers lost money? Those don't sound like very good odds to me!" For starters, we don't know exactly how many people have actually lost money in the stock market. After all, they're not going to brag about their crucifixion on Penn Central, are they? So let's concentrate on *why* a person loses. There are two basic reasons. Either he doesn't have a sensible plan or, and this is more likely, if he has a plan he doesn't have the nerve to stick with it. But probably *the overriding reason for failure in the stock market, or in any speculative market, for that matter, is that it's too easy to let the crowd do one's thinking.* I guarantee this: if you act on all the completely logical, obvious reasons for doing something, you'll lose your money, your pride, and probably your sanity in short order, because you'll virtually never do the right thing. Why's that? Well, if a certain fact, or step, is obvious to *you,* don't you think it's just as obvious to everyone else? And don't you think they've already done something about it—like buying or selling *before* it became so obvious? You can bet your pet toad on it! If a "reason" is already widely known, it's no longer worth acting on: the prevailing market price already includes everything that's known to everyone, so it's too late for you to move!

"O.K., so what does that have to do with why most people lose money?" Remember the sunbelt affair? Most people need to have an obvious reason before they plunk their money down. Thus, when the evening newscaster effervesces about improving economic conditions, the crowd is logically putting it together as higher profits, higher dividends, and higher stock prices to come. But stock prices already reflect what's known. So the crowd is going to have to wait for still better news before they see any more price rises. And there's a limit to how good the economy can get, just as we hope there's a limit to how bad it can get! As a general rule, most people fail because they buy too late, just when things look their best, just when the market is reaching its peak. (It's not any coincidence that stock prices reach their top *before* the final peak in an economic boom. That's happened so often that stock prices are included in the government's series of leading economic indicators.) After buying too late, people compound their mistakes by going into a panic when, months later, the headlines go on about the bleak news coming out of Washington and Wall Street. And then we have panic dumping of stocks by the same people who bought when everything looked super! It's sure defeat if you join in with the current thinking (if you can call it that) of the masses! Given the crowd's amazingly consistent record of snatching short-term capital losses (what the hell, they're deductible!) from what should have been long-term capital gains, is it any wonder they've quit the stock market in droves?

We can't afford not to invest our money in the stock market because the odds of winning, and winning big, are so high! Even if we had no plan, if all we had was the presence of mind not to panic along with the crowd, our chances of making our fortune are better in the stock market than in any other investment media we've talked about. When we develop a sensible game plan, we'll do even better than the summary statistics shown in Table 6-2. Here you see the investment results we'd

Table 6-2. Total returns from all NYSE common stocks for 1926–1975 (percent per year compounded).

	1-Year Periods	2-Year Periods	3-Year Periods	4-Year Periods	5-Year Periods
$1/6$ returns over	44.3%	34.2%	29.1%	25.9%	22.8%
Average return	13.3	11.9	11.2	10.8	10.7
$1/6$ returns below	−18.7	−10.4	−6.7	−4.3	−1.4
Percent showing profit	60	73	75	81	80

	6-Year Periods	7-Year Periods	8-Year Periods	9-Year Periods	10-Year Periods
$1/6$ returns over	20.7%	19.4%	18.4%	17.6%	17.4%
Average return	10.6	10.9	11.3	11.4	11.5
$1/6$ returns under	0.5	2.4	4.2	5.2	5.6
Percent showing profit	82	86	88	95	95

	15-Year Periods	20-Year Periods	25-Year Periods	30-Year Periods	35-Year Periods
$1/6$ returns over	17.1%	16.3%	15.7%	14.8%	13.7%
Average return	11.8	12.2	12.3	12.1	11.5
$1/6$ return under	6.5	8.1	8.9	9.4	9.3
Percent showing profit	100	100	100	100	100

have achieved if we'd simply bought stocks and hung on for the indicated periods during the fifty years we've been using as a reference. This fifty-year period, remember, includes the Great Crash as well as the lousy markets of the late 1960s and the early 1970s—in short, the best and the worst of what has happened—and it forms an excellent reference for what we can expect in the next fifty years. And unless one wishes to argue against overwhelming evidence, there are several extremely important inferences we can draw from these numbers.

    1. Stocks are *risky!* There's a chance, particularly in short spans of time, that you would be hard-pressed for an answer if you had to explain why you were investing in the stock market. In fact, the odds of making any money at all in any single one-year period are only 3:2 in your favor—not very good betting odds. But look what happens if you're willing to let it ride for five or ten years. The betting odds improve from 3:2

to 4:1 to 19:1 in your favor. At horizons of fifteen years and beyond, it's nearly certain that you'll make some money . . . but how much?

2. Stocks are *profitable!* You can expect to earn, on the average, at least 10% per year compounded. At 10% compounded, your $100 a month turns into nearly $200,000 in thirty years. And if you get the normal 12% return for thirty-year periods, your $100 a month becomes a cool $290,000. In fact, there was only one case in this entire fifty-year period where the thirty-year compound return was less than 7½%— it dropped all the way to 7.4%. And there were *no* cases where the thirty-five-year compound return was less than 7½%. Even under the worst conditions, $100 a month at 7½% for thirty years grows to around $125,000. Best case? A little over 15½% for thirty-year periods, and then $100 a month swells to just over $575,000. How's that?

Remember one thing. We're not talking about picking the next IBM here. These are average stocks! Not just the big winners, but the big losers too. In fact, these numbers include *every stock* that was listed on the Big Board between 1926 and 1975—the ones that are today's corporate giants, the ones that went bankrupt, and the ones that were just plain there. In other words, what these figures show you is exactly what you or I could have achieved without any plan, without any research, armed with nothing but the presence of mind not to panic when the news got bad. *With* a plan, you can expect to do considerably better than the 10% to 12% average return. Incidentally, these figures include reinvestment of dividends and the cost of brokerage commissions as well. They don't include taxes, so they're comparable to all the other return data we've cited. Unlike savings accounts or bonds, where you have to pay taxes on your interest earnings each year, common stocks, like real estate, are tax-favored. Again like real estate, common stocks can be leveraged to increase the total return to you.

Just as a clincher, in Table 6-3 we've ranked each of the major investment media according to our criteria for selection with triple weighting for expected *real return* because it's so vitally important to us. We've used a scale ranging from 0 for

Table 6-3. Ranking of investment media. (0 = awful, 5 = great. Real returns weighted triple.)

Media	Expected Real Return Over 10 Years	Risk of Capital Loss Over 10 Years	Ability to Diversify on $100/Mo.	Tax Advantages	Liquidity	Total
Treasury bills	0	5	5	0	5	15
Cash savings	3	4	5	0	5	17
Insurance	1	4	5	3	3	15
Bonds	6	3	5	2	4	20
Mortgages	9	4	0	0	0	13
Real estate	12*	4	0	5	1	22
Stocks	15*	2	5	3	4	29

*Tax advantages and leverage can improve after-tax real returns.

awful to 5 for *great;* anything beyond that is gravy. Then we've combined the scores to indicate their relative attractiveness. No question about it: it's the stock market hands down! And now that we're convinced of that, and we've seen its hazards, and we know its rewards, we've got to get down to the serious business of mastering the inherent risks and maximizing the potential returns.

We'll tackle that next.

Why a
Mutual Fund?

IF you like money as much as I do, you must have been nearly mesmerized by the numbers in Table 6-2. In fact, you may be ready to run out and buy a few shares of something that will fly through the next decade. That's a lot easier said than done! There are over 2200 different stocks listed on the New York Stock Exchange, another 1200 or so on the American Stock Exchange, and thousands more in the over-the-counter market. So how are you going to know which one will be next year's winner? You don't! But you've got lots of company. The fact is, no one knows which ones will scream and which will bomb.

There are stock-pickers at your brokerage firm, stock-pickers who'll sell you a subscription, and stock-pickers who run mutual funds. Every one of them will analyze all the financial data and come up with all the obvious reasons why their favorite *must* go up—and they'll all get uniformly rotten results! In a good year, they'll do as well as the market indexes, and a few may even do a little bit better. But the vast majority won't do as well as you can on your own. You'll save some commissions and/or subscription fees, and you'll probably do better than the experts if you'll just put your own noodle to work.

The problem of how to play the market really comes down to two basic decisions. *Which* stock should I buy or sell? *When* should I buy or sell it? If those sound like simple questions, keep in mind that no one has found a guaranteed answer to either of them in the last hundred years. And we certainly can't count on the canned labels—growth, glamor, or whatever—to give us much help, since a company's characteristics may change overnight. But if we understand the problem, maybe there's a way we can reduce the range of necessary decisions to a manageable proportion.

Let's attack the problem of which stock to buy or sell first, since it's the easier question to deal with. In fact, we'll find that it's the single most compelling reason for depending on a mutual fund. Start by imagining yourself sitting across the desk from an account executive at the local brokerage firm. The broker will tell you all the facts you'd ever want to hear about Bullhead Catfish Company: how the research analyst looks favorably on the firm's prospects, how the earnings have grown steadily for years, how the balance sheet looks strong, how the company's management is well-trained and aggressive. He'll give you answers to everything you *don't* need to know. And he'll gloss over the only two things you do need to know: First, what's the expected return? That is, what capital changes (changes in the price of the stock) and what dividends can you look forward to? And second, how much risk do you have to take? Since you're the person who is plunking down your cold, hard cash on this little gem, you've got a right to know what the chances are that you'll lose your marbles. Of course, if you ask such questions as "How much can I make?" and "How much can I lose?" point blank, you'll catch him off his guard. His initial response is likely to be something incomprehensible about Bullhead's net working capital position. But remember what's important. You don't really care whether Bullhead Catfish can pay its creditors or not, *you care about what's likely to happen to the price of its stock and what kind of dividends you're going to get.* That's all!

Keep after him. About the third time you ask your two questions—"How much return?" and "How much risk?"—you should be able to pin him down. After all, he's quite capable of visualizing a commission flying out the window unless you get an answer. Eventually, he'll put his expertise on the line, with something like "I expect it to go from $20 to $25 in the next year, and then there's the $1 dividend." You're on the right track—you've forced half an answer out of him. Now you can put together the 25% expected capital gain and the 5% expected dividend for an expected one-year total return of 30% . . . not that shabby! O.K., now to the tough question. How much risk? Ask him what he thinks it might sell for under these two extremes—if everything goes absolutely right, and if everything goes completely wrong.

"If everything goes right," he'll start happily, "you know— bull market, good earnings, lots of investor interest—there's maybe one chance in a hundred that this honey could go up to $30." How *about* that?! A possible 50% gain (dividend excluded) under the best of circumstances. How about the worst— bear market, bad earnings, and other such untoward surprises? "Well," he sours, "I guess it could go as low as $10, but it would sure be a bargain there." Ugly . . . a possible 50% loss (dividend excluded again) in a bear market. That's kind of scary. But you're out to compare stocks. You're shopping around looking for the best buy exactly as you'd shop for a new car or a stereo, and now you've got the necessary information. Let's put it on a graph. Chart 7–1 shows the expected return (we've dropped the dividend return for simplicity) in percent on the vertical axis and the range between extremes— 100%—on the horizontal axis. Since that one dot looks so lonely out there, let's repeat the process and get the same kind of estimates for some other stocks. Then let's pull all the new dots on the same chart for comparison. Eventually, you'll be able to pick the stocks that have the highest expected return for any given level of risk . . . in other words, the best buys. That's a rational way to shop.

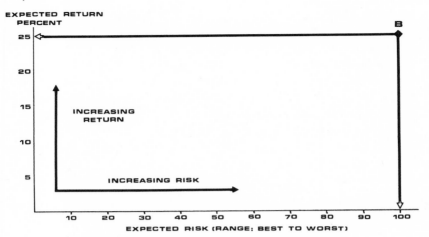

Chart 7-1. Expected return and risk, single stock.

By this time, you've driven the broker bananas; but he's getting accustomed to your routine. You keep plugging away and he keeps giving you his estimates of upside potential, downside risk, and dividend payments. By the twentieth stock or so, you can begin to see a pattern emerging. Generally—not always, but as a rule—you'll find that the return figures he estimates for you are increasing as the risk exposure increases. You already knew of the direct relation between higher risk and higher return; now you can see it on your own graph, Chart 7–2.

The fact that expected return rises as you take more chances is extremely important to your long-term wealth-building program. It tells you that you ought to concentrate your investments in the riskier stocks usually traded on the American Exchange and in the over-the-counter market. In theory, as we've said, you should be able to do considerably better over the long haul than the 10% to 12% historic return from New York Stock Exchange stocks simply by accepting more risk when it's necessary! But remember: if it's not necessary to take a risk, and if it doesn't pay—if you don't get paid extra for taking it—don't take it!

In addition to the direct relationship between risk and return, you can see that some stocks are clearly better buys than

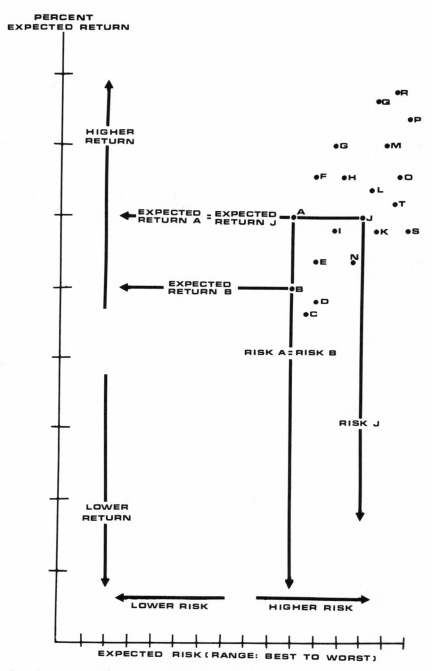

Chart 7-2. Expected return and risk, 20 stocks (A to S).

others. On chart 7–2 stock A is clearly superior to stock B, since A has a higher expected return than B with the same risk exposure. Stock A is also better than J since it has the same expected return but with less risk. In general, stocks above (higher return) and to the left (lower risk) dominate the others. Since you want higher return but you want to avoid taking unnecessary risk, you'd pick A, F, G, Q, or R, since they offer the best returns at their level of risk. So let's concentrate on these five.

Well, we've narrowed things down quite a bit. We're down to picking our favorite issue out of just five. But we've got some hesitation about putting all our eggs in one basket. And just as we're considering a combination of two or three stocks instead of just one—presto, we find another amazing feat of academic magic. Look at Chart 7–3. If we choose two or three stocks and combine them into a portfolio, the portfolios are usually superior—that is, they offer higher returns for equivalent risk—to any of the individual stocks! What happened? Essentially, the good surprises on some stocks—higher-than-anticipated earnings, unexpected dividend increases, and so on—cancel out the bummers. We've diversified our investments and, if we include enough stocks, we'll completely eliminate the shocks that can hit an individual company from time to time.

"All right, that's a neat trick, but how many stocks does it take to get rid of the unnecessary risk completely? After all, I can't go out and buy twenty or thirty stocks—the commissions would eat me alive!" But that's exactly what you have to do if you're going to use the market to its fullest advantage. You either pay the commissions (a horrendous drain on your $100-a-month capital) or you can go out and buy a market index like the Standard & Poor's Composite which contains 500 stocks—it's one of those "efficient" portfolios which gives maximum return for a specified level of risk. Virtually all mutual funds hold twenty or thirty stocks; some have several hundred. So when you own a mutual fund, you own the market. Don't let that point get lost! Unless you have an awfully good reason to think that you can pick stocks better than the professional analysts, the most efficient, most easily affordable, and

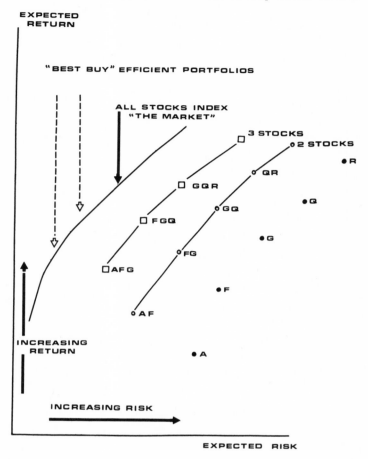

Chart 7-3. How diversification reduces risk.

least expensive way that you can participate in the stock market is through a mutual fund.

The conclusion we've just reached, that the market index is one of the superior portfolios, is the primary reason so many mutual fund managers have moved toward indexing the portfolios they supervise. In fact, some mutual funds intend to duplicate exactly the composition of the major market averages, usually the S&P 500 Composite, owning exactly the same stocks in exactly the same proportion. A mutual fund, then, is half of the answer you want: it eliminates the stock selection problem. We'll deal later with the question, "When should I buy or sell?"

"O.K., I'll settle for a mutual fund instead of trying to pick out individual stocks, but now I've got the problem of which mutual fund. I mean, there are about six hundred out there, so how do I know which one to use? They're not all alike, are they?" No, they're not all alike. But most do have at least one characteristic in common—they move in the same direction as the market. (A few specialized funds that concentrate heavily in particular industries can move against the broad market, but they're the exception rather than the rule.) Some funds move more slowly, some move faster—but practically all move in the same direction as the market.

And since 600 is a pretty unwieldy number, let's use the process of elimination to narrow our choices. First, we can eliminate the load funds! There's absolutely no sense in paying a sales commission of up to $8^3/4\%$. Load funds have absolutely no performance advantage over no-load funds— very simply you *don't* get what you *do* pay for. Next, we can eliminate the closed-end funds. These are publicly traded, as stocks are. And like stocks, you pay a brokerage commission to buy or sell them. An unnecessary expense, especially since these funds aren't even traded at their true asset value! That fact reduces the tendency of the closed-end fund to follow the market, which unnecessarily complicates our decision. So the closed-end fund is out. Finally, we can eliminate those funds that concentrate their portfolios in particular industries, such as gold, chemicals, or oils, since they may or may not follow the market well.

And now, as a result of all this culling, we've reduced the list of acceptable funds from over 600 down to about 150 or so no-load investment companies. These 150 will have to be pared still further before we get down to the final selection. In addition to diversification, which ensures that the fund will move in the same direction as the general market, we'll want our no-load to have rather high concentrations of American Stock Exchange and over-the-counter issues for two important reasons: probable growth and probable volatility. Since most of tomorrow's "established" growth stocks are currently brand-new companies with brand-new ideas and products, they haven't made it to the Big Board yet. With the risks in the unseasoned AMEX and OTC issues obviously greater, the potential rewards are too. These stocks are also likely to be much more volatile than the NYSE issues, which are far more widely owned. Both growth and high volatility will prove to be extremely valuable to us, as we'll see.

So our final decision on which fund to buy—we'll actually need three or four to do the best job—should be based on the following criteria.

Diversification. This practically eliminates the chance of picking a loser when the broad market is rising. It is the most important advantage mutual funds offer.

Low trading costs. In a no-load fund, 100¢ of every investment dollar goes to work for us; none of our money is diverted to compensate the sales staff.

Expected return. By looking for funds that concentrate on AMEX and OTC issues, we ensure both the probable growth and the probable volatility of the fund. Both these factors increase the return we can expect on our money.

The No-Load Mutual Fund Association (Valley Forge, PA 19481) will provide, free of charge, a listing of currently registered no-load funds categorized by the fund's investment objective. Under normal circumstances, we'd be looking for an "aggressive growth" fund. A fund's prospectus and its past performance are important guides to its aggressiveness, which has a lot to do with its expected growth and volatility. It's not unusual for some funds to move up and down two or three times faster than the market. As we'll soon see, the faster the better!

Once our small group of no-loads has been selected (we'll hone the selection process in Chapter 11, but you should write for that listing from the No-Load Mutual Fund Association now and have it ready) we've effectively eliminated the "which stock" decision. We're left with the entire market. And we can expect our fund to do essentially what the market indexes do—go up and then go down as the speculative cycle changes. We can also expect it to grow over the long term.

Back in Chapter 6, we spent a bit of time looking at figures on the rate of return for all NYSE stocks over the fifty-year period from 1926 to 1975. We found that it was quite reasonable to expect a total return of around 10% to 12% per year just for being willing to accept the market's risk. Now let's take a closer look at what we can expect from the stock market. We've actually got over a hundred years worth of hard numbers to play with, so we can come up with a pretty accurate picture of the vehicle we've chosen for our wealth-building program.

Most of the stock market graphs you're likely to see leave out about half the total return from stock investments because they don't include the dividend income the stocks paid. And too many charts bias their results by choosing time periods designed to make certain other investments look better by comparison. Chart 7-4 is an example of a chart that might be used by a commercial bank in an attempt to lure your investment dollars into a savings deposit. In Chart 7-4, you're looking at one of the *worst* ten-year periods (as measured by the Dow Jones Industrial Average) in the last century, and you're looking at a slanted comparison. In other words, you're looking at a salesman's gimmick.

Chart 7-5 shows a fair comparison of the same $1000 investment for the same ten-year period—one of the worst ever for stocks, remember. This chart includes dividends received and the results of their reinvestment. The important difference is the *after-tax returns.* You have to pay taxes every year on all the interest your bank pays, but you pay none on capital gains from the stock market until you sell your stock, and even then the dividend income goes at least partially untaxed. Even in those ten dismal years, most investors would have done better in the market than in the bank!

A fair comparison over a longer period of time, Chart 7-6, shows why wealthy people prefer to own stocks. If one of your beneficent forebears had put just $100 into a broad list of stocks in 1871, reinvested the dividends received along the way without adding one extra nickel, that $100 would have grown to nearly $180,000 by 1971, and to nearly $220,000 by the end of 1976. The banker would have done very poorly by you, accumulating only $3980 after the first hundred years

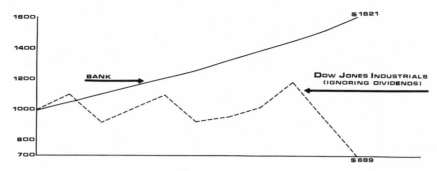

Chart 7-4. A misleading comparison of stock and bank investments.

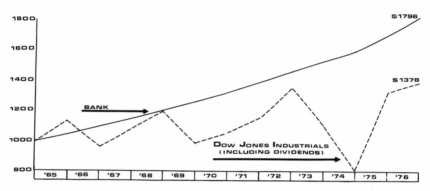

Chart 7-5. A better comparison of stock and bank investments.

and only $5128 after a hundred and five. What a difference!
You can buy a new Ford Pinto with the bank's $5000. Or you
can swing a Bentley, a place on the beach in La Jolla, and a
mountain retreat in Aspen, and still have $5000 pocket
change if your great-granddaddy was bright enough to put
that $100 in stocks. Throughout the 105-year period, stocks
yielded over 7½% per year compounded annually, compared
to only 3¾% for savings accounts. Sure, your money's safer in
a bank—but how much are you willing to give up for safety's
sake?

   "Hey, I thought you were talking about 10% or 12% long-
term in the stock market, not 7½%! What kind of razzle-daz-
zle is this?" You caught that, did you? Well, the discrepancy
arises primarily from the market measure we're using to de-

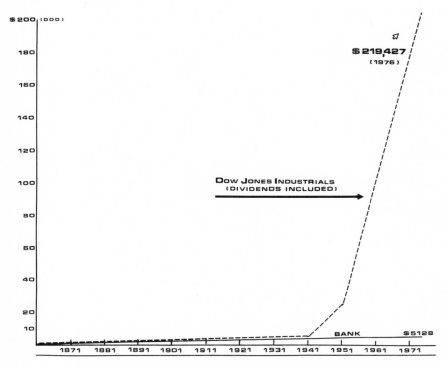

Chart 7-6. The long-term comparison of stock and bank investments.

scribe the action of all common stocks. For the 105-year study, we've had to splice together two different indexes describing the price movement in what is today the very highest-quality (lowest-risk) segment of the market. In the 50-year study, we were using all stocks listed on the New York Stock Exchange between 1926 and 1975. Let's compare the two measures, the Dow Jones Industrial Average representing the highest-quality stocks, and the unweighted indexes which include all NYSE stocks, good, bad, and average. The results you can see in Table 7-1. Over the long haul, you see that the typical stock usually outperforms the top quality issues. There we have it again—higher risk, higher expected returns.

Simplify things. Let's try to set a realistic standard we can rely on to estimate the future. To begin with, let's scratch the Roaring Twenties and the Depression that followed it. People

Table 7-1. Measuring the market: total returns per year for the Dow Jones Industrial Average vs. the unweighted NYSE Index (1926–1975).

	Dow Jones Industrial Average	NYSE Unweighted All-Stocks Index
Compound rate of return 1926–1975	7.9%	9.9%
Average of 41 10-year periods	8.4	11.5
Average of 35 15-year periods	8.5	11.8

can't speculate in stocks as wildly now as they could prior to the Great Crash, when they could get a piece of the action for only 10% to 20% down. Economic conditions have changed (hopefully for the better) since then, and it's unlikely that we'll have to go through that kind of nightmare again. Then, since we don't have very good comparative data for the period prior to the 1920s, let's slice that off, too. That leaves us with about forty years—let's say 1938 to 1977—to use as our reference. Since more detailed data are available for the Dow Jones Industrial Average than for almost any other stock market index, we'll use it—keeping in mind, however, that it *understates* the actual expected return by two or three percent a year, since it represents the lowest-risk sector of the stock market.

In Table 7-2 we've listed the total return for the Dow Jones Industrial Average for each year in our yardstick. That in-

Table 7-2. Annual total return for Dow Jones Industrials: capital changes with dividends reinvested. December averages, 1938–1977.

Year	Return	Year	Return	Year	Return	Year	Return
1938	24.5%	1948	3.3%	1958	33.1%	1968	9.8%
1939	3.3	1949	17.9	1959	19.7	1969	−16.9
1940	−6.7	1950	22.5	1960	−8.0	1970	5.8
1941	−8.6	1951	21.1	1961	22.1	1971	7.9
1942	11.4	1952	11.9	1962	−9.4	1972	18.7
1943	19.0	1953	1.7	1963	19.3	1973	−18.2
1944	17.0	1954	44.5	1964	16.1	1974	−25.6
1945	32.8	1955	26.4	1965	11.9	1975	43.2
1946	−7.1	1956	3.8	1966	−14.4	1976	18.2
1947	7.6	1957	−8.4	1967	12.8	1977	−12.1

cludes changes in market price plus dividends reinvested at the time they're received. When we average these out, we find that a reasonable expectation is a little less than 10% per year. We see, too, that there's a strong wave action at work in the stock market, each cycle averaging a little over four years in length. To learn how to take advantage of it, we're going to be looking at the market at least once every month, not just every December. Based on monthly data for the Dow Jones Industrial Average, we can come up with an adequate measure as our reference for the future (Table 7-3).

Table 7-3. Total return: Dow Jones Industrial Average. Monthly mean prices, 1938–1977. Percent per year compounded.

	1-Year Periods	5-Year Periods	10-Year Periods	20-Year Periods
$1/6$ of returns over	25.4%	14.8%	14.3%	12.5%
Average return	9.7	8.7	9.4	9.5
$1/6$ of returns under	−5.8	2.6	4.5	6.5
Percent showing profit	73	86	97	99+

Now let's try to make some sense out of the numbers. Again, we see that total return on this index generally runs around 9% per year and that as time goes on, the investment results smooth out: the effects of the market cycles diminish. Let's really concentrate on the mid-range expected returns, since all we need are average results to run our $100 a month to over $7000 in five years and maybe $20,000 after ten years. And remember, this index understates what we should really get, since it's the lowest-risk segment of the stock market! We can reasonably expect to add at least another percentage point

Table 7-4. Expected value of our $100-per-month investment.

	5 Years	10 Years	20 Years
Using Dow Jones Industrial Average (1938–1977) [average value]	$7,100	$18,600	$65,100
Using average-quality NYSE stocks (1926–1975) [average value]	$7,500	$20,600	$86,500

or two to our annual rate of return just by going after somewhat lower-quality stocks: that is, stocks that offer higher risk.
In round numbers, Table 7-4 indicates what we should expect
our $100 a month to do for us based on past experience.

Now that we know what we're playing for, let's get on with
the plan.

How to Get It
and Keep It
Without Even Trying

WE'RE ready to start investigating two formulas for timing your investments. These formulas are designed to force you to take the proper investment strategy without any application of brainpower, without that "when do I buy or sell?" headache. But since they don't require any expertise on your part, one thing's certain: they won't improve your returns much in the long run. The probability that you'll get rich without effort is, after all, roughly the same as the probability that you'll win a million at blackjack. Our primary reason, therefore, for discussing these formula plans at all is to separate their good points from their shortcomings. In the next chapter, we'll combine the best elements of the two in a skeletal structure for an improved and workable investing method.

You already have one big advantage over wealthy people.

For a few years, you'll be able to face bear markets without
fear of losing all your assets. Falling prices will simply present
you with another opportunity to pick up bargains. Whether
the market is in a bullish upward trend or headed straight
down, you'll be forced to do the right thing with your
money—just as long as you don't lose your nerve.

The first of the formula plans we'll talk about is called
Dollar Cost Averaging. It's a mechanical rule that says, Buy
more shares near the lows and fewer near the highs of the recurring cycles in stock market prices. Dollar Cost Averaging
has been around for a long, long time for one reason: it
works. It's a method that guarantees you'll at least keep up
with the market over most five- to ten-year periods. It forces
you to buy most heavily right at the bottom of a bear market,
just when everyone else is losing his cool and bailing out in
panic. Unfortunately, it doesn't guarantee that you'll make
money. But the odds are better than 9:1 that you'll make some
profit if you follow the plan for five years and over 30:1 that
you'll show a profit if you hang on for ten years. Those are
pretty fair betting odds, and they're good because you're taking advantage of the cycle.

We've already seen that cycles in stock prices last approximately three to five years. Although there are considerable
variations in cycle length, we can probably expect to see two or
three complete bull market/bear market sequences in most
ten-year periods. Obviously, what we'd really like to do is buy
all our shares right at the final bottom of the downward swing
and then sell out at the ultimate top of the next speculative
cycle. But it can't be done. There's absolutely no way known to
man to accomplish that neat little trick. So let's check our
dreams of quick riches and try to do the next best thing. How
about buying a large number of shares near the bottom and
not buying too many near the top? That's exactly what Dollar
Cost Averaging is designed to force us to do.

To explain the operation of this scheme, we'll need a typical stock market cycle to work on. If we measure the cycles of
the last hundred years, we'll come up with something that
looks like Chart 8-1, which is fairly representative of major
stock market trends over the past century. There are two

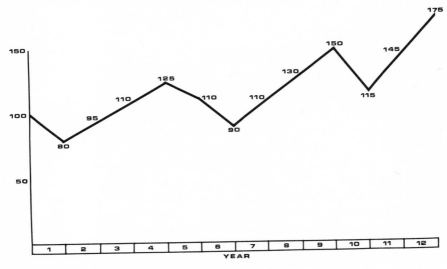

Chart 8-1. Typical stock market trends.

major components in this longer-term pattern. First, there's a secular (20- to 50-year) growth trend that causes the overall level of prices to increase at about 4$^{1}/_{2}$% a year. Second, there's the purely speculative cyclic component, that three- to five-year span from trough to trough or peak to peak. We've disregarded dividends—normally another 4$^{1}/_{2}$% or so for a total return of around 9% on the Dow Jones Industrials—so this example doesn't reflect the return we can really expect. That lets us keep it clean, so that we can see Dollar Cost Averaging at work.

Of course, the perfect answer would be to buy low and sell high. But we're only buying under this plan, so that we never have to pay taxes on the gains. The best we can hope for, then, is to *buy more when prices are low* and to *buy less when prices are high.* And that's the essence of Dollar Cost Averaging: how to get it at the lowest average cost. In a Dollar Cost Averaging plan, we simply invest a fixed number of dollars each week, month, or year *regardless* of the market's level or trend. In other words, we're admitting to everyone that while we haven't the foggiest notion which direction stock prices are going to move next month or next year, we do expect the

long-term direction to be up, as it has been for the last two
hundred years.

Let's assume that we stash our $100 a month in a savings
account and then invest it at the end of each year. That's
$1200 a year into the market regardless of how good or bad
we think things are. There's the formula part of the Dollar
Cost Averaging plan; we don't necessarily need any brains,
just the nerve to follow through. So what happens?

What happens is that our $1200 buys more shares of stock
when prices are low and fewer shares when prices are high, as
we see in Table 8-1. To get the number of shares you've purchased in any one year, simply divide $1200 by the price
index. Then add that to the total of all the shares you've accumulated in prior years, multiply that by the current market
price index, and you have the current market value of your
holdings. If you compare the market value to your total cost,
you can determine your profit or loss. Your profit or loss position has a considerable psychological impact on your will-
ingness to continue with the program; we'll get around to that
point in just a second.

*Table 8-1. Dollar Cost Averaging: hypothetical results using the stock market
index.*

Year	Price Index End of Year	Amount Invested This Year	Shares Bought This Year	Total Shares Accumulated	Market Value of Total Shares	Total Invested	Total Profit or (Loss)
0	100						
1	80	$1,200	15.0	15.0	$ 1,200	$ 1,200	—
2	95	1,200	12.6	27.6	2,625	2,400	$ 225
3	110	1,200	10.9	38.5	4,240	3,600	640
4	125	1,200	9.6	48.1	6,018	4,800	1,218
5	110	1,200	10.9	59.0	6,496	6,000	496
6	90	1,200	13.3	72.4	6,514	7,200	(686)
7	110	1,200	10.9	83.3	9,162	8,400	762
8	130	1,200	9.2	92.5	12,028	9,600	2,428
9	150	1,200	8.0	100.5	15,078	10,800	4,278
10	115	1,200	10.4	111.0	12,760	12,000	760
11	145	1,200	8.3	119.2	17,289	13,200	4,089
12	175	1,200	6.9	126.1	22,066	14,400	7,666

On paper, the Dollar Cost Averaging method looks pretty fair. The results shown in Table 8-1 are just about what you could expect if you averaged into the stock market over a period of ten years or so. Not very dramatic, but you would have accumulated around $20,000 you wouldn't have had otherwise. Essentially, what you have done here is to plug into the long-term growth in equity prices, and take a little—very little—advantage of the cyclical changes in speculative demand. You can see that Dollar Cost Averaging is only a method for getting started in the investment process. You're making only about 7½% per year here without counting dividends—not fantastic, but you *did* get off to a good start. The point is that you've accumulated a $20,000 stake on $100 a month without having to sweat it. Incidentally, you've paid zero taxes on your capital gains; you've had no capital gains, since you've sold nothing.

There are a few refinements we should make in this Dollar Cost Averaging process. As a general rule, the more often we put our money into the market the better our investment results will be. Why? One, because we're using no-load funds, so there are no commission costs to fret over. And two, because we're getting closer to the market cycle: we're buying many more shares near the lows in the market and far fewer shares near the highs. You'd be using the Dollar Cost Averaging method to just about its maximum benefit if you were to make monthly contributions: one check each month to pay yourself first. Paying into the program on a monthly basis as opposed to a once-a-year basis probably gains you another ½% to 1% or so in total return per year. Not much, but take every edge you can get when it's free.

"Sounds good in theory, I guess, but does it really work?" Fair enough question; let's look at the investment results Dollar Cost Averaging has produced in the past. Over our forty-year reference period, from 1938 to 1977, it would have accumulated the final dollar amounts shown in Table 8-2 on an investment of $100 a month. These results clearly show that you can't expect a Dollar Cost Averaging program to work miracles. Over the long haul, it should outperform an unmanaged portfolio by maybe 1% to 2% per year. There is a

Table 8-2. Results of Dollar Cost Averaging: total returns on an investment of $100 per month using the Dow Jones Industrial Averages for 1938–1977.

	5-Year Plans	10-Year Plans	20-Year Plans
⅙ of plans over	$8,861	$25,448	$102,319
Average plan	7,564	19,951	72,620
⅙ of plans under	6,267	14,454	42,921
Percent showing profit	91%	97%	99+%
Total contributed:	$6,000	$12,000	$ 24,000

real problem with Dollar Cost Averaging, though, and it's this.

After a few years, what happens to the fifty or hundred shares you already own becomes a lot more important than the cost of the new shares you're buying in any month. In other words, the formula doesn't protect the shares you acquired last year or two years ago from bear market slides. Once you've got $5000 worth of stock, the negative effect on your total wealth of, say, a 20% cycle drop ($5000 × .2 = $1000) would more than completely offset the advantage of any extra shares you might get on your $100 purchase near the trough. So we have to accept the fact that Dollar Cost Averaging, while good in theory, is only practical for very short periods of time, usually a few years at the most, while you're getting your feet wet in the investment process. So let's find a better way.

"Something better? What's that?" Well, we know that the whole purpose of the averaging scheme is to take advantage of cycles in the stock market—to buy more shares at low prices and fewer at high prices. But bear markets of 25% to 30% or so didn't really force us to buy that much more stock at low prices, and bull markets that gained 75% or so didn't force us to buy that much less at high prices. In other words, the market's cycle just isn't strong enough to cause big shifts in the number of shares we're buying every month. If we had a *huge* cycle, Dollar Cost Averaging would work a lot better. But where do we get a big cycle?

You remember those aggressive no-load funds we talked about? Some of them really take off when the market's headed up . . . maybe three or four times as fast as the Dow Jones Industrial Average. On the other hand, they fall like a rock in a bear market. But the point is: between the two extremes they give you a gigantic cycle ride. So if you've got the nerve to follow through, you should end up buying tons of shares at very low prices near the trough and buying fewer and fewer shares at high prices approaching the peak. Let's go back to Chart 8-1, pick up the typical market cycle pattern, and then magnify it by using a high-volatility fund. To make the point that high volatility is absolutely essential, I've stretched the cycle more than is possible in actual practice, although we *can* come close. Keep in mind that your fund will invariably move in the same general direction as the market because it's diversified (a market effect portfolio), but it'll move an awful lot faster than the market in percentage terms. So its cycle might look like Chart 8-2.

We've exaggerated the cycle, but we've assumed that our fund's overall long-term growth during the twelve-year period is the same as that of the general market. Therefore, any improvement in return will reflect one thing: the use of a fund that moves, and moves fast. Here goes.

Let's compare the results of the Dollar Cost Averaging program on the high volatility fund, Table 8-3, with the same scheme using the stock market index, Table 8-1. As you'd ex-

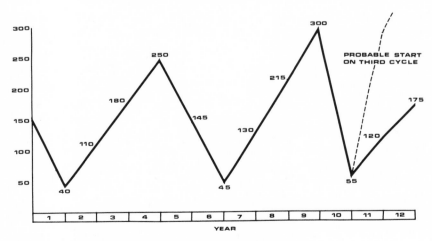

Chart 8-2. Magnified cycle effect, high volatility fund.

Table 8-3. Dollar Cost Averaging: hypothetical results, $100 a month invested in an extremely volatile fund.

Year	Price Index	Fund Price	Invested This Year	Shares Bought This Year	Total Shares Accumulated	Market Value of Total Shares	Total Invested	Total Profit (Loss)
0	100	$100						
1	80	40	$1,200	30.0	30.0	$ 1,200	1,200	—
2	95	110	1,200	10.9	40.9	4,500	2,400	2,100
3	110	180	1,200	6.7	47.6	8,564	3,600	4,964
4	125	250	1,200	4.8	52.4	13,094	4,800	8,294
5	110	145	1,200	8.3	60.7	8,795	6,000	2,795
6	90	45	1,200	26.7	87.3	3,929	7,200	(3,271)
7	110	130	1,200	9.2	96.5	12,551	8,400	4,151
8	130	215	1,200	5.6	102.1	21,958	9,600	12,358
9	150	300	1,200	4.0	106.1	31,839	10,800	21,039
10	115	55	1,200	21.8	127.9	7,037	12,000	(4,963)
11	145	120	1,200	10.0	137.9	16,554	13,200	3,354
12	175*	175*	1,200	6.9	144.8	25,341	14,400	10,941

*Assumed equal in order to compare results.

pect, there's a far greater risk of holding a losing position—sometimes even a painful position—when you're using the high volatility fund. But you can also see that the magnified cycle made you buy huge quantities of shares at low prices and only a microscopic number at high prices. The end result is that you'll wind up with more shares if you use the high volatility fund. And except for bear market years, you'll show far higher profits on your investment dollars. In the five to ten years of wealth accumulation ahead of you, high volatility will work greatly to your advantage as long as you don't quit near the bottom of a bear market!

Why would anybody quit just when he knows he has a chance to pick up bargains? Good question. All of us court pleasure, and all of us abhor pain, right? Any time you're dealing with money, pleasure and pain are almost exclusively determined by past results—your profit or loss position at any point in time. One of the many quirks of our species is that we like to double up when we're winning—on the theory, no doubt, that if one drink makes us feel good, another will make us feel even better. Look at the profit position in Table 8-1 or Table 8-3. When are profits best? Right smack at the top of the speculative cycle. Given man's tendency to proclaim his own genius as loudly as possible at the most inauspicious moment possible—when he's winning big—he'll want to toss even more money into the program near market peaks. That, of course, is just the opposite of what he should be doing, and it utterly destroys the effectiveness of the Dollar Cost Averaging method.

Even worse is what he does when he's losing. Can you imagine having to defend a $5000 loss (as in year 10, Table 8-3) to your friends? If you then wanted to throw another $1200 down that hole—good money after bad—they'd think you were absolutely insane. As a practical matter, it takes an incredible amount of courage to continue investing under this plan during the final throes of a bear market. You will have lost around half your chips, the headlines will be rotten and getting worse, and you'll be catching a lot of flack from anyone who knows you're in the market. The "sane" thing to do would be to escape, to quit. And that's exactly what most people do. They duck, they run for cover, they listen to the crowd. They lose perspective and they blow it. Believe me, if you keep on plunking your money down the first time the market heads south after you have started this thing, you've got guts.

So much for Dollar Cost Averaging. Let's highlight its strengths and shortcomings. Dollar Cost Averaging does force us to accumulate more shares when they're cheap and fewer when they're overpriced. From that standpoint, it does provide a service by making us do the right thing in bear markets. Even if we had absolutely no knowledge about what the future might bring, it'd be pretty hard for us to go badly wrong with a Dollar Cost Averaging plan unless we picked lousy stocks (which is unlikely in a mutual fund) or we quit the program when the news got bad. I repeat: we can expect to lose if we allow our emotions to override the automatic investment strategy. Greed, the temptation to buy and buy, is always present after we've done well, when we can see that things are good, and when everyone else expects things to get even better; just as fear, the temptation to sell out, always sets in when past efforts have turned sour, when things are generally considered to be bad, and when the crowd expects them to get even worse. To make any investment program work, *we must stick to the plan.*

As for its shortcomings, we've already mentioned the important one. The limiting defect of the Dollar Cost Averaging method is that it doesn't do anything to protect the dollars we've already accumulated. After we've spent years building a portfolio of $5,000 or $10,000, it can really hurt to sit through a 20% or 30% slide while we hang on to our package of volatile funds. So we'd better find some way to protect the money we've already got.

Protection is what we'll deal with now. How are we going to cover ourselves against a rout? Ideally, we should have all of our investment capital in cash right at the top of the cycle, sit on it for the entire bear market drop, and then go to a full equity commitment—100% of our money in stocks—at the absolute bottom. We have to find ways to approach that ideal, to keep ourselves from being fully exposed at market tops. Now our emphasis has changed from *getting* money—capital accumulation—to *keeping* it—capital preservation. How do we do it? We keep part of our money in the bank and the remainder in the market, depending on the market condition. That way, we have extra cash on hand to snatch up stocks when they're cheap, and we never have all our money exposed to the next crash. But the big difference now is that, whereas Dollar Cost Averaging required us just to buy and hold, now we *buy and sell according to a strict formula.*

That formula is probably the most popular mechanical rule for protecting wealth, once you've got it, against severe market slides. It's known as the Constant Ratio plan. The name is derived from the fact that the total wealth you've accumulated is to be divided into two risk classes: first, aggressive assets like stocks; second, defensive assets like cash. Each of these groups is then held as a fixed percentage of your total portfolio value. In theory, the aggressive assets (stocks) should be sold off as their prices rise or bought when prices are falling, to maintain the specified ratio. Under the Constant Ratio plan, we should be selling stocks during periods of bull market strength and buying them back during periods of bear market weakness. Again, it's a purely mechanical system that doesn't require that we know where stock prices are going next month or next year. Here are the rules.

Depending on how much market risk you're willing to accept, you select a ratio—that is, a percentage of your accumulated assets—which will be constantly committed to stocks. That's your aggressive part. As a defensive move, and for use at bargain time, the remaining portion is committed to cash. For example, someone with a very low tolerance for risk might choose a ratio of 20% stocks to 80% cash. Twenty to 80 is an extremely defensive, low-risk way of putting some capital to work in the stock market, but it doesn't offer much improvement over the bank rate. (Remember: low risk = low return!) We need a degree of protection, but without quite so severe a restriction on our overall earning rate. So for us, a higher commitment to common stocks is more appropriate: a stock-to-cash ratio of 60 to 40, 70 to 30, or 80 to 20. Unfortunately, the choice is arbitrary; it's completely up to you. Let's try an example to see how it works.

Take another look at Chart 8-2. We'll use the same magnified cycle in our package of volatile funds and apply the Constant Ratio plan to $5000 we've already got, using a stocks-to-cash ratio of 75 to 25. The Constant Ratio principle can also be applied to stocks of normal volatility, but remember, the stronger cycle of the aggressive funds will pay off in more money at the end. In virtually any market, we'll be better off with a portfolio partially invested in aggressive no-loads and a cash reserve on the side than we would be with a portfolio fully invested in stocks of normal volatility.

Using the 75 to 25 Constant Ratio, we are going to maintain a constant 75% of our total assets in the market, with the remaining 25% in a defensive cash reserve. At the start of the program, therefore, we'll put $3750 (0.75 × 5000) into our mutual fund, and the remaining $1250 into a savings account at, let's say, 5% interest per year. Table 8-4 will indicate the terrific advantage of having a cash reserve on hand with which to pick up bargains in a bear market. It's a little difficult, how-

ever, to understand at first. So let's walk through it step by
step. We started with $5000 allocated between stocks ($3750)
and cash ($1250). At the end of year 1, our aggressive fund is
down a disastrous 60%—an atrocious start. We have only
$1500 left in stocks ($3750 × .4). This, unfortunately, is when
most people run—and it's precisely when they *shouldn't*. We've
also got a cash reserve, after a year's 5% interest, of $1313
($1250 × 1.05). So now, the total value of our portfolio is
$2813 ($1500 + $1313). But remember our 75 to 25 Constant
Ratio! Of that $2813, $2110 ($2813 × .75) ought to be in
stocks; only $703 ($2813 × .25) ought to be in cash. Our desired position, $2110 in stocks and $703 in cash, is quite different from our actual position of $1500 in stocks and $1313
in cash. So the Constant Ratio formula tells us to purchase
$610 worth of stocks at the end of year 1, in order to *bring our
actual position in line with our desired position.* If we can keep our
wits when everyone else is in a fright, we'll almost always buy
after prices have fallen sharply, and we'll sell after they've
risen rapidly. That's what the plan is forcing us to do.

After we've done our $610 worth of buying, we start year 2
with a portfolio of $2110 in stocks and $703 in cash. And

Table 8-4. 75 to 25 Constant Ratio plan.

Year	Price Index	Stock Value	Cash	Total Value	In Stocks (75%)	In Cash (25%)	Action Required	
		Actual Position at End of Period			*Desired Position*			
0	100	$ 3,750	$1,250	$ 5,000				
1	40	1,500	1,313	2,813	$ 2,110	$ 703	buy $	610
2	110	5,803	739	6,542	4,907	1,635	sell	896
3	180	8,030	1,717	9,747	7,310	2,437	sell	720
4	250	10,153	2,559	12,712	9,534	3,178	sell	619
5	145	5,530	3,337	8,867	6,650	2,217	buy	1,120
6	45	2,064	2,328	4,392	3,294	1,098	buy	1,230
7	130	9,516	1,153	10,669	8,002	2,667	sell	1,514
8	215	13,234	2,800	16,034	12,026	4,008	sell	1,208
9	300	16,780	4,208	20,988	15,741	5,247	sell	1,039
10	55	2,886	5,509	8,395	6,296	2,099	buy	3,410
11	120	13,737	2,204	15,941	11,956	3,985	sell	1,781
12	175	17,436	4,184	21,620	16,215	5,405	sell	1,221

thanks be, year 2 goes a little better for us. Magnifying the market's rise, our fund roars to a year-end value of $5803 [$2100 × (110/40)] and our cash account grows by another 5% to $739 ($703 × 1.05) for a total value at year's end of $6542 ($5803 + $739). Since our fund has shot up so rapidly, we've now got more exposure to the market than our Constant Ratio would dictate: we should have only $4907 in stocks ($6542 × 0.75) and $1635 in cash. So at the end of year 2, we'll sell off $896 worth of our fund shares, and we'll be back to our 75 to 25 ratio. Since we make these necessary changes at the end of each year, the cyclical market effects apply to the desired stock portfolio, not the end-of-period stock value. For the same reason, it's the *desired cash position* that will be earning interest in the following year.

"Hey," you're saying, "if those numbers are right, we've hit a jackpot. We've quadrupled our money in twelve years and we haven't held a losing position since the sixth! And we haven't put in a buck in the process. Can that really happen?" Well, yes and no—how's that for an answer? Yes, in theory— if. If we have the nerve to buy more stocks after a start that would make most people quit. If we have the nerve to sell just when everything looks good, when most people would be buying. And if we can find a fund as volatile as the fund we've been using here as an example. Even if we could completely control our nerves (and that's hard to do when our stocks are down 60%), we'd be hard pressed to find a no-load fund that gained over 500% in a bull market and lost more than 80% in a bear market. A few currently registered no-loads come close to that kind of volatility, so when we're choosing our funds we'll search for the screamers—fully aware that they'll completely bomb in one year out of every three or four.

Both Dollar Cost Averaging, which accumulates our base of investment assets, and the Constant Ratio, which protects them, are designed around the assumption that cycles in stock prices will continue to occur. And on the basis of the hundred-odd years' worth of market data we've got, there's a strong indication that cycles will be around for years to come. Cycles are caused almost completely by changes in speculative demand. Until the masses learn to temper their emotions, we can expect a continuing string of bull markets followed by bear markets, superimposed on a long-term upward trend. And the stronger each cycle is, the better the results will be for both the Dollar Cost Averaging and, more particularly, the Constant Ratio plans. It's vital, therefore, that we find some highly volatile no-loads if we're to get the most out of any cycle with either formula.

You've seen that it's important for us to have a cash reserve that we can use to grab stocks at bargain prices. You've also seen that our ideal is to be completely *in stocks* near bear market bottoms, and almost completely *out of stocks* near bull market tops. We'd get the best of the upside ride on our volatile fund, and we'd miss most of the crushing drop. If we could do that, we'd be sitting pretty in ten or twenty years. While we can't expect perfection, we can come close enough to make the attempt worthwhile—and we'll see how in the next chapter. But before we press on, a brief recap. Here's what we've covered so far.

We need to have financial goals. Now that we know it's possible to gain financial independence on just a few bucks a day, it's time to drag out our financial statements, list our net worth, our projected income, and our foreseeable needs, and try to decide realistically how much money we want to have in ten or twenty years. Then we decide how much we can afford to pay ourselves each month. We set the highest figure we can, and we determine to pay ourselves *first* every single month.

We need high rates of return. We don't want to take unnecessary risks, but we do have to invest where we can expect our money to work hardest for us. We know that the after-tax real returns from savings, insurances, bonds, and most mortgages are so low they're not even worth considering. Emergency cash and necessary insurances, yes; investments in safe, fixed-income media, no! That means either real estate or common stocks.

We need diversification to spread the risk of picking the one loser in a rising market. No-load mutual funds allow us to accumulate a diversified portfolio of stocks on $100 a month, even less in some cases, but we're effectively priced out of the real estate market until we can afford to hold several different parcels.

We need high growth and high volatility. In order to get the benefits of faster-rising capital values over the long haul, we'll concentrate our attention on those no-load funds that invest primarily in smaller growth stocks. They're the most volatile, and their expanded cycle effect generally improves the investment results in the long term. Used with a rational plan that tells us when to accept the stock market's risk and when to step aside, high volatility aggressive growth funds are the best all-around vehicle for wealth building.

A rational plan that tells us when to play and when to hide. That's our next goal.

How to Get More
and Keep More—
with a Little Effort

WE'VE just talked about two extremely simple devices—Dollar Cost Averaging for accumulating money, and the Constant Ratio formula for protecting it. And we saw that neither required any brainpower on our part. In both schemes, we follow a robot-like approach to the timing of purchases and sales. The DCA and CR rules will take advantage of the cyclic nature of market prices as long as we follow their dictates. And both methods do produce some improvement in long-term returns. But how about applying some intelligence to the problem?

Let's start with the premise that the Lord didn't stuff the space between our earlobes with cabbage. If we're lucky, He gave us the capacity to think our way through to a better solution. So if we're willing to put our heads to work, we can probably combine the most useful parts of these mechanical plans. First, let's develop a theoretical framework for getting money and keeping it. We'll deal with a few of the practical problems and their solutions later on.

The name of our combined method for accumulation and protection is Variable Ratio, and it does exactly what its name implies. It varies the ratio between stocks and cash in accordance with the cycle condition. The Variable Ratio has essentially the same purpose as the mechanical plans: to cash in on the long-term uptrend of stock prices, and to benefit sharply from the recurring cycles. But it goes about buying and selling much more aggressively and intelligently than do the simple formulas. We'll also find that it's relatively easy to modify the basic Variable Ratio method so that it produces a big improvement in returns with considerably lower risk than we face in either of the purely mechanical schemes. That combination—higher potential earning rates and reduced exposure to loss—is the payoff if we can get the method to work in practice. Let's start with the structure of a Variable Ratio plan and see what's supposed to happen.

Again we'll need a typical speculative stock market cycle to work on, so let's go back to Chart 8-1. But this time let's remove the factor of long-term growth, so that all we see is the cycle itself, as in Chart 9-1. Now keep in mind that without the long-term secular growth trend, we're looking at *price level changes only*. In other words, both elements of profit— dividends and long-term appreciation—are gone, so we're working with just the *speculative cycle*. Obviously, it's not nearly this smooth or regular in real life, a practical problem we'll have to deal with later on. But it's about what we'd get if we measured the stock market cycles of the past century. It's close enough to the real world for our immediate purpose, which is to indicate how the Variable Ratio method works.

One look at Chart 9-1 and you can see that the bullish upward phase usually runs from the low 70s to somewhere around 100, where it reverses to a bearish downward trend that typically carries back again to the low 70s. "Well, why don't we just buy in the low 70s and sell in the high 90s? We'll make money hand over fist!" Great idea in theory, but it has

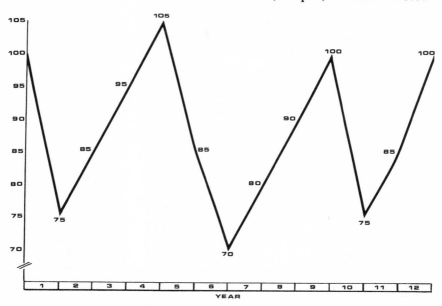

Chart 9-1. Cycle component of prices; no growth, no dividends.

its practical problems. Did you think you were the first person ever to figure these cycles out? There are other investors who've come down the same road. And if there were enough of them, and they all decided to do something about it, there'd be a huge number of potential buyers (added demand) in the 70s and an awful lot of potential sellers (added supply) in the 90s. The added buying pressure in the 70s would keep the cycle from ever reaching its former bottom. By the same line of reasoning, the added selling pressure in the 90s would keep prices from ever reaching their former top. In other words, if everyone knew about the cycle, they'd eventually adjust their buying and selling habits to take advantage of it— that additional buying at lower prices and the additional selling at higher prices would diminish the amplitude of the cycle! Eventually, there would be no cycle left at all—just dividends and long-term growth.

But we know they can't *all* have figured it out; too many investors still buy when the headline news is good and still sell when the news is bad. So there are bound to be future cycles, though they're not going to be as smooth or regular as our example pretends. This is just a hypothetical cycle we're using to analyze the structure of a Variable Ratio plan.

As we said, we'd really like to be fully invested in stocks when prices are near a cycle low, and be out of them entirely and into interest-earning, no-risk cash when prices are near a cycle high. But since the cycles are rather irregular, we're faced with two unanswerable questions: "How high is high?" and "How low is low?" We can't ever know with absolute precision, so let's try establishing our investment position in gradual stages. We'll move toward a more fully invested position as prices approach their former cycle lows, and we'll reduce our exposure to a market slide as prices approach their former cycle peaks. In other words, we'll vary the proportion of wealth we've committed to equities. As the cycle changes, we'll change the ratio of stocks to cash: we'll hold a high ratio of stocks to cash near the former cycle troughs, and a very low ratio near former cycle peaks. In short—a Variable Ratio.

Let's assign an arbitrary percentage of our total investment capital to the market at the former cycle limits. We realize that future cycles won't match past ones exactly, but our operating assumption is that they'll match sufficiently well to enable us to make a profit from trading any given cycle. O.K. We see that the historic center line has been around 85. So let's pull a number out of the air and say that near the cycle center 50% would be appropriate: a 50 to 50 ratio of aggressive assets like funds to defensive assets like cash. We'd like to be fully invested (100% of our assets in the market) by the time the cycle reaches its low and completely out (0% invested in stocks) at the high. Also let's leave ourselves some slack by getting progressively closer to the 100% position as prices approach the region of their former cycle lows (arbitrarily, 60% stocks at 80 and 80% at 75). Let's take the top end in stages too. We'll get closer to the 0% point as prices move toward former cycle highs (again arbitrarily, 40% stocks at 90 and 20% at 95). What we've done here is to divide the range between past highs and past lows into six roughly equal segments. The number of divisions, of course, is a matter of choice. We could just as easily have used ten divisions or two.

Since the Variable Ratio plan will become the basis of our final wealth-building program, I think it only fair that we understand exactly what's happening. So let's walk through the numbers in Table 9-1 carefully. The most important feature is this: we'll be building a low-risk cash reserve as market prices move above the center line and as they continue toward their ultimate peak. By the time they reach their speculative top, we should have stockpiled a huge cash reserve; with a minimum in stocks, we'll have a very low exposure to market risk. Conversely, as prices fall below the center line into bargain territory, we'll be using our large cash reserve to pick up stocks while they're dirt cheap. The presence of an ample cash reserve—ideally 100% of our total assets near the peak—allows us to buy much more aggressively when prices are low than would Dollar Cost Averaging. By the same token, the Variable Ratio forces us to sell much more aggressively at high prices than would the Constant Ratio, since now our desired commitment to stocks decreases as price levels rise. At least in theory, we've built a better structure than Dollar Cost Averaging for accumulating shares: our larger cash reserve is used for progressively larger and larger purchases at lower and lower prices. And it's a better structure than the Constant Ratio for protecting wealth: a higher percentage of our total wealth is held in cash reserve when prices are high.

Since it's superior to Dollar Cost Averaging for getting money, and it's superior to the Constant Ratio for keeping money, we can use the Variable Ratio plan whether we're starting from scratch on $100 a month or already have a substantial stake. Just to make sure we all understand the following example, let's walk through the Variable Ratio method using our hypothetical market index. Assume that we've got $1000 to start with, but that we're not making the $100 monthly contributions. We'll put them together later on when we test this method against actual stock market experience. But for the time being, let's keep it clean.

We're ready to go with $1000 in cash after we've measured our cycle limits over a long period of time (year 12), and here comes tomorrow, future year 0. Again we're assuming that we can get 5% on our cash balance.

Table 9-1. Hypothetical investment results for a Variable Ratio plan.

Future Year	Actual Position at End of Period				Desired Position				Action Required
	Price Index	Stocks	Cash	Total Value	% in Stocks	$ in Stocks	% in Cash	$ in Cash	
12=0	100	—	$1000	$1000	—	—	100%	$1000	none
1	110	—	1050	1050	—	—	100	1050	
2	85	$ 454	1102	1102	50%	$ 551	50	551	buy $ 551
3	70	—	579	1033	100	1033	—	—	buy 579
4	95	1402	—	1402	20	280	80	1122	sell 1122
5	80	236	1178	1414	60	848	40	566	buy 612
6	65	689	594	1283	100	1283	—	—	buy 594
7	85	1678	—	1678	50	839	50	839	sell 839
8	100	987	881	1868	—	—	100	1868	sell 1868

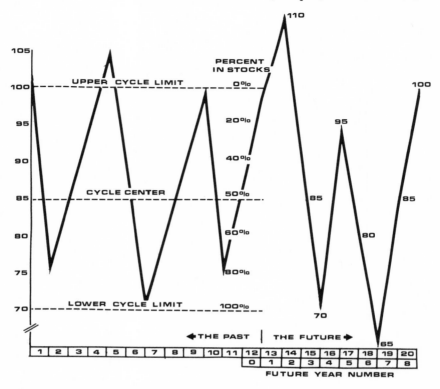

Chart 9-2. Cycle limits and investment ratios.

The technique is the one we learned under the Constant
Ratio plan. *All we have to do is to rearrange the actual composition
of the portfolio (the percent of assets in the market and in cash) at the
end of each year to bring it into alignment with the composition dic-
tated* by the Variable Ratio plan. Let's see how we do it. We'll
start on December 31 of year 0 with the market index at 100.
Looking at Chart 9-2, we can see that the 100 level has
marked several cycle *peaks* in the past, and our Variable Ratio
dictates a completely defensive position at the peak: 0% stocks,
100% cash. So we put our $1000 in the bank and hold it there
for the full year at 5%.

This time we're fooled. The market continues to climb
another 10% in year 1. We were wrong, but our money is safe.
At the end of year 1, we've got our $1000 starting capital plus

the $50 interest earned (let's ignore taxes). And the Variable Ratio still points to a completely defensive position. So we'll leave our $1050 in the bank through year 2 and let it earn another $52 interest.

The speculative bubble breaks during year 2 as stock prices fall nearly 23% to 85. We're looking a bit less idiotic; we decided not to leap into the market with both feet last year when the crowd wanted in on the action, and we weren't so dumb after all! We're sitting on an accumulated wealth of $1102 ($1050 + $52 interest earned during year 2). Now the Variable Ratio indicates that we ought to be 50% in stocks and 50% in cash, since the market index is on its center line. O.K. We'll switch half of the cash reserve into fund shares—$551 in stocks and $551 in cash going into year 3.

Dammit, wrong again! (Accept it. It happens.) The market falls once again in year 3 to close at 70. We've taken a 17.6% (70/85) loss on our fund shares. Now they're worth only $454 [(70/85) × $551]. But we've still got $579 sitting in the bank ($551 + $28 interest earned in year 3). And here's where we test your mettle. The Variable Ratio says we're so close to the bottom that we ought to use it all to buy more fund shares. Remember what we said earlier about psychology? And why people quit when there are bargains around? Well, we—you— just took a pretty hefty loss last year. How do you feel about plunking another $579 into this bummer? Even if it seems like the stupidest thing you could conceivably do, *do it!* What the hell, if all the sayers of doom are proved to be right for a change, and the world does come unglued, $579 isn't going to mean much, is it? Buy another $579 worth of fund shares (now you've got $1033 on the line) and pray a lot.

Whew! The Good Lord came through just in time! Stopped the rain, quelled the oceans, and pulled off another miracle to save planet Earth once more. You had it all hanging out last year, and now you're a financial wizard. Your fund shares went up almost 36% in one year, and you're up more than 40% since you started, even though the market is still down! But it's time to start getting cautious again, since the market index is above its center line. Do some selling to bring your actual portfolio, now $1402 strong, into the recommended 20 to

80 ratio. As you go into year 5, keep just $280 (.2 × 1402) in fund shares, and keep a large $1122 (.8 × $1402) defensive cash reserve.

That's the first complete cycle, so let's look at results. Overall, the market hasn't gone anywhere for four years. (We eliminated the factors of dividends and long-term growth, remember?) Actually, market prices are still 5% below their starting level, but you've got a rather substantial 40+% profit. How'd that happen? It happened because you were cautious. Cautious enough to know when prices were too high, when it was time to run for cover. *And* because you were gutsy! Gutsy enough to plunk your money into the market even though you were scared. Any time you *aren't* scared, you're more likely to lose. O.K., that's it; I've stroked your ego enough. It wasn't all your genius, you know. The Variable Ratio had something to do with it. Take it step by step through the second full cycle now, until you're completely comfortable with the way it works. And don't forget to keep psychology in mind. You started this scheme four years ago with $1000 flat. Have you ever been far behind? That makes the method a little easier to live with, doesn't it? Now try to second cycle on your own.

There are a couple of very favorable attributes of the Variable Ratio plan we ought to look into. Most important is the fact that this strategy forces us to buy more aggressively when prices are low by historic standards and it forces us to sell more aggressively when prices are high. Since we invest more and more dollars at lower and lower prices, and take more and more dollars out of the market at higher and higher prices, we've come much closer to taking full advantage of the cyclic moves. Keep in mind that we haven't even considered dividends or secular growth yet. Remember, too, that we don't expect future cycles to be exactly like past cycles, just reasonably similar. There will be times when we'll be completely out of the market even though prices are still rising; we have to expect that we'll miss the speculative tail end of some bull markets. Nobody knows where the ultimate peak of any cycle is, but there's a point at which it just isn't too smart to play for the last few dollars, when there's too big a chance the market will drop out from under us. On the downside, too, there will be a few times when we'll feel the pain of a loss position because we bought in too soon. Accept the fact that on occasion we'll miss the ultimate top by getting *out* too soon and the final bottom by getting back *in* too soon.

But—and here's the payoff—by taking the fullest possible advantage of the cyclic swings, we can expect to get a much higher return with significantly lower risk exposure. We've tied our investment strategy to an important question: "Is the market too high or too low?" So all we need are, first, a reliable gauge of cycle limits, and second, the center line between them. We'll have to do some brainstorming to get those measures, but we'll find that there are some pretty decent guidelines we'll be able to follow. We'll get to that real-world problem in a while, but let's play around with the basic Variable Ratio plan and see if there's anything we can do to improve it. A couple of things leap to mind.

Obviously, the bigger the cycle, the more effective the plan (remember our high-volatility no-loads). If we take Chart 8-2 and forget about growth and dividends, we get the high-volatility fund cycle shown in Chart 9-3—magnified, but essentially the same as our market index. In addition, we've assumed again that there are no differences in final values. Thus, any difference in the results we achieve is due exclusively to our high volatility fund rather than to the market index. Since the cyclic swing of our hot fund is roughly twice as great as that of the regular market, we'll adjust our percentage invested ratios to allow for the enlarged movement (dividing the past range into just five equal segments) and we'll get the results shown in Table 9-2. Run through the numbers, and then compare the final wealth for this example with the results achieved using the market index, as shown in Table 9-1. Now do you see why I've been harping on aggressive no-loads?

"Wait a minute, Hayes, it can't be *that* easy!" You're right. We've made quite a few assumptions that don't exactly work out in the real world. We've assumed cycles that swing back and forth with great regularity between predictable limits, and no-load funds that move three or four times as fast as the

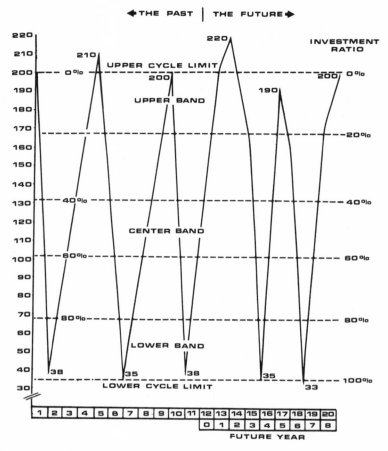

Chart 9-3. High volatility cycle limits and investment ratios.

market. No, it's not that easy at all. But if we can deal even roughly with the problem of cycle limits when we go into the real world, this Variable Ratio plan should put us way ahead. We'll soon see that it works, and can work well, because the method forces us to be aggressive buyers on low prices and aggressive sellers on high prices.

We're ready to press on to the practical problem of finding some reference that will tell us whether the current cycle condition is too high or too low. First, though, let's add a couple of refinements to the structure of our Variable Ratio plan.

Table 9-2. Hypothetical investment results for a high volatility fund using the Variable Ratio plan.

| Future Year | Price Index | Fund Price | End of Period | | | Desired Position | | | | Action Required |
			In Stocks	In Cash	Total Value	% in Stocks	$ in Stocks	% in Cash	$ in Cash	($ Worth of Stocks)
0	100	$200	—	$ 1,000	$ 1,000	—	—	100%	$ 1,000	none
1	110	220	—	1,050	1,050	—	—	100	1,050	none
2	85	170	—	1,102	1,102	20%	$ 220	80	882	buy $ 220
3	70	35	$ 45	926	971	100	971	—	—	buy 926
4	95	190	5,271	—	5,271	20	1,054	80	4,217	sell 4,217
5	80	160	888	4,428	5,316	40	2,126	60	3,190	buy 1,238
6	65	33	438	3,350	3,788	100	3,788	—	—	buy 3,350
7	85	170	19,514	—	19,514	20	3,903	80	15,611	sell 15,611
8	100	200	4,592	16,392	20,984	—	—	100	20,984	sell 4,592

One of the refinements has to do with when we start using the Variable Ratio to buy or sell. Another is a *simplification* that reduces the amount of grunt work required to manage the plan in practice. Let's attack the question of *when*.

As I've said, where we place the investment ratio bands or how many bands we use is completely arbitrary. For example, we could take the past cycle range and divide it up into ten or twenty bands, or even more, as in Chart 9-4. But no matter how many investment bands we choose, the basic Variable Ratio plan always had us buying too soon (as soon as prices began to come down from their peaks) when it would have been wiser to postpone our buying until prices were even lower. So let's institute some *halfway rules*. First rule: no buying until prices have come down to their center line! The percentage commitment to the market will now be as it appears over year 6. That modification should keep us from buying into a falling market when there's a high degree of probability that

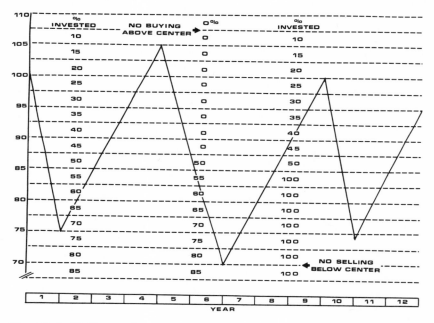

Chart 9-4. Halfway rule.

prices will continue to come down quite a bit more. Under the basic plan, we always ended up selling too soon (just as prices began to rise from their cycle lows) when it would have been smarter to hang on and wait for higher prices. So another halfway rule: no selling until prices have risen above their center line. Now the investment ratio varies as you see it over year 8, when the market is rising.

As a practical matter, the guides we'll eventually use to determine cycle limits and center line are rough—very rough indeed. Using ten or twenty investment ratio bands, therefore, implies a numerical precision we just aren't going to find when we try to put this plan into practice. We'd only be kidding ourselves if we expected future cycles to fit past cycles perfectly, so we can do nearly as well in the real world by using only a few investment ratio bands, as in Chart 9-5.

Now we've got a modified Variable Ratio plan with only four or five investment bands to worry about. That's quite enough to force us into buying stocks more heavily only when they're underpriced. As a result, most of our purchases will be made near cycle lows, and that should significantly improve the investment returns we get. Also, since we'll be selling stocks only after they've risen sharply, we'll be building our cash reserve near peaks to protect our wealth from the next slide.

"What if the next slide, or the next rise, for that matter, doesn't come?" It will; sooner or later it will. And if it's a slide, we'll be sitting through most of the bear market with our money intact, ready to pick up the bargains next time around. "Well, how about that middle ground where stocks are fairly priced—why aren't we doing something there?" Because they're priced just about where they should be. That's enough to give us the 9% or 10% fair return for accepting market risk, but not enough to lure us into committing our cash reserve. We want the promise of a higher return before we use our cushion. Still, it's enough to keep us interested in stocks until the expected return gets too low. So until the market tells us what to do by moving one way or the other, we don't buy and we don't sell. We just hang on to the investment position we've taken and expect to get a fair return on that. Eventually, the

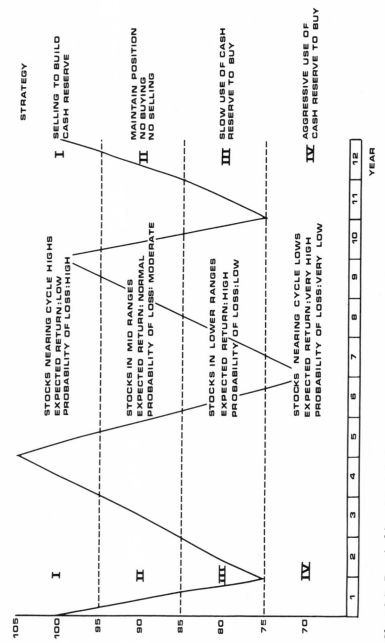

STRATEGY

I SELLING TO BUILD
CASH RESERVE

II MAINTAIN POSITION
NO BUYING
NO SELLING

III SLOW USE OF CASH
RESERVE TO BUY

IV AGGRESSIVE USE OF
CASH RESERVE TO BUY

STOCKS NEARING CYCLE HIGHS
EXPECTED RETURN:LOW
PROBABILITY OF LOSS:HIGH

STOCKS IN MID RANGES
EXPECTED RETURN: NORMAL
PROBABILITY OF LOSS: MODERATE

STOCKS IN LOWER RANGES
EXPECTED RETURN: HIGH
PROBABILITY OF LOSS:LOW

STOCKS NEARING CYCLE LOWS
EXPECTED RETURN:VERY HIGH
PROBABILITY OF LOSS:VERY LOW

YEAR

Chart 9-5. Practical investment strategy.

market will move, and we'll be ready to do the right thing: buy underpriced or sell overpriced.

Before we get into sticky real-world problems, one note of caution about *nerves*. Every time our Variable Ratio plan directs us to do something, all the headline news will be telling us to do exactly the opposite. That's exactly why we can expect our plan to do better than average. Near market peaks, all the news will be euphoric and every mini-speculator between Buffalo and Bakersfield will want a piece of the action. The smartest thing we can do then is to let them have our share at retail. After the next cyclic break and near the final trough, all the headlines will be sour, and the amateurs will want out because they got hurt. That's when we take a deep breath, step in, and take it off their hands at wholesale. It's happened every four or five years during the last century, and it'll happen again. It's up to us to have the patience and the nerve to follow the plan!

Now let's see if we can't find a reference we can use to estimate cycle limits.

What Price
Should You Pay
for Value?

ALL we need to complete our Variable Ratio plan is some reasonably reliable reference for figuring out whether stocks are steals (that is, underpriced), dangerous (overpriced), or fairly priced. Once we've solved the problem of the cycle limits and the center line, we can develop a set of tactical operating rules and test them against market data to see if they've worked in the past. There's no guarantee that because a system has worked in the past it will work in the future. But it would be a strong indication that we were on the right track. And you can bet that if an investment scheme has not done well in the past, there's almost no chance that it will provide much guidance in the future. So we're looking for some sort of reference that fills two requirements: it *has worked* in the past and it *has theoretical justification,* which rules out mysticism.

142

There are a thousand places we could look for a reference, so let's not waste time. Let's look in the right place first. "Fair enough. What's the right place?" Value, *intrinsic worth,* is what establishes the investment demand for any asset. We recognize, of course, that there's a separate speculative component that is always at work, and that can and does drive actual market prices either above or below their true values. But it's the intrinsic, or fair, value of an asset that establishes the center-line reference we need for our plan. In the case of common stocks, the factor that determines their value is the income stream they provide to shareholders. And the income generated by common stock arises from two primary sources: dividends and growth. So if we want to know whether common stocks are underpriced, overpriced or fairly priced on an investment as opposed to a speculative basis, we'll have to try to relate prevailing market prices to the income the stocks provide.

Let's take a look at the income stream we can expect to get from a hypothetical stock. Maybe it'll tell us why stocks don't always sell for a price that's fair. Say I buy a stock for $20 and it pays me a 90¢ dividend during the first year. That's a current dividend yield—one component of income, remember—of $4^{1}/_{2}\%$ in the year. That probably doesn't sound too shrewd, since I could have done better today by socking my twenty bucks into a savings account. But I wouldn't have bought the stock in the first place if current dividends were all I cared about. I paid a fair price for the thing because the company's economic situation seemed to me to be favorable, and I thought the dividend would grow. And growth, as I've said, is the second component of income.

Just for the sake of argument, let's say I was right. The company's business gets better during the second year I own my share, and the company's directors raise the dividend from 90¢ to 95¢. The stock becomes even more attractive, and investors bid its price up to $21—still a fair $4^{1}/_{2}\%$ yield to prospective buyers. But the price rise catches the eye of a few speculators who spot the obvious reason, that increased dividend. They're saying to themselves, "All right, what happens a few years down the road after the dividend has grown to

$1.25? That little hummer should be going for around $28, assuming it continues to yield $4^1/2\%$, and it's only $21 now. I think I'll buy some!"

You can see what's happened. Speculative demand has entered the price determining process. The added demand created by the first round of speculators has driven the price up a bit, say to $23.75, to yield 4% on the current 95¢ dividend, and that bump has attracted the attention of a second round of speculators, and before you know it, a trend is in the making. "Hey!" the second-round speculators are saying to themselves. "That company's growing, and it will probably be paying a $1.30 dividend a few years from now." (Note that in order to get moving, they needed a somewhat more optimistic projection of future business prospects than did the first-round speculators.) Based on a current yield of 4%, considered fair by the new speculators since that's the market now, they decide that "this honey could sell for $35 to yield 4% on expected future dividends of $1.30 in a couple of years. It's under 24 now, so maybe I'll buy some!" The added dose of speculative demand kicks prices up another notch, say to $28.50, and the company, which has had another good year, raises its dividend to $1 a share.

A speculator's dream come true: rising prices confirmed by good news! The current dividend yield is only $3^1/2\%$ ($1.00/$28.50 = 0.035) but never mind—our baby's growing like a weed! As for me, I've got a good profit at this point— better than 50% in two years—and if I'm even half smart I'll be out beating the bushes to find a potential buyer for my share. Luckily for me, here he comes. And he's chanting, "It's been going up and it's bound to go up more. After all, it's a growth stock, isn't it?" Who am I to disagree? I just go ahead and sell it to him.

At this stage in the cycle, the Greater Fool Theory is in full operation. Nobody's bothering to analyze or keep things in perspective. They're just rushing to buy this newly discovered growth-glamor issue. New buyers are paying far too much now, because they honestly believe there will be somebody who'll pay even more for it later. In one final surge of speculative demand, the market price soars to $35—less than a 3%

yield to current buyers—before the unexpected news comes out. The company's business was just about the same this year as it was last year, and the dividend will remain at $1.00 a share for the foreseeable future.

What good is a growth stock that isn't growing? Not much. If it's only going to pay a buck a share for the next few years, it ought to be selling in the low-20s, not the mid-30s. Step aside as a new rush starts; with expectations unfulfilled, the smartest speculators start selling: The new supply created by their dumping forces prices down. And falling prices warn the second round of speculators that the trend has changed from bullish to bearish. They bail out, and the new onslaught of speculative supply causes even more rapid declines in the market prices. So goes the cycle.

The point is that it's speculative demand, not intrinsic value, that causes most stock price changes. If you think I've stretched this example just to prove it, I haven't, not one bit. Actually, there's no reason our baby blue-chip couldn't have continued to ride the speculative tide for a year or five years or even more. That's happened to literally hundreds of growth stocks before. Levitz, the furniture retailer, is a good case in point. One of the bona fide screamers during the heyday of any-price-for-growth, it leaped from $7 to over $240 a share in less than four years—a bubble filled with wild expectations of never-ending earnings increases. The bubble exploded in 1972 before the onset of the recession, and the stock plunged to $6 a share when earnings plummeted and black ink turned to red. (In the for-what-it's-worth category, Levitz paid its first dividend ever, 20¢ a share, in late 1977—ten years after the joyride got started.)

I don't mean to single out any one stock as a destroyer of dreams; hundreds, maybe thousands of stocks over the years have been guilty. There's almost no limit to how high a given stock can climb at a given time, provided it's in vogue, and everyone's playing Greater Fool. The problem is that there's also no limit to its *fall* when all those overblown expectations fail to materialize. So maybe I was foolish for bailing out of that stock I owned at $28.50; after all, it could have gone to $50, or $70, or $700. For any single stock, it's absolutely impossible to know how high the top is, or where the bottom may be. For stocks in general, though—and I mean all of them, the up-and-comers, the mature institutional grades, and the old-age decliners—there's a pretty good, if imperfect, way to tell whether they're outrageously overpriced or bargains. It's a rough, imprecise gauge that will tell us whether the market is too risky or dirt cheap, so we'll know whether to plunk down our money or not. And it'll help us make a lot more money on our investments when we do decide to play the game.

Do you know any good poker players? Watching a high-dollar table is one of life's finer educational experiences. We've all heard about the guys who make a living just by playing card games skillfully. I'm not talking about the minor-league dudes who roll into the game to get in on the action; they're playing for the excitement, and they're likely to leave most of their chips on the table when they quit. I'm talking about the pros who generally take home a bigger stack at the end of the game than they had when they began. The strange thing is that most of the time it's the same guys who win big.

If you watch a serious game for a couple of hours, you'll notice something different about the way the winners conduct their business. They're no different in the way they look, or dress, or talk, and the cards they get aren't materially better. What differs is the way they play their cards. They don't ante up in every pot; they ante up, in fact, in surprisingly few pots. The winners bet heavily only when the odds are in their favor, and they fold when the odds are against them. They're consistent winners primarily because they recognize when the odds are good and when they're not, and they place their bets accordingly. So here's your operating rule. The better the odds, the higher your bet! When the odds are against you, fold! Sure, you may pass up a few pots. But it's absolutely certain that you'll have more chips at your corner of the table when the game turns your way again.

Exactly the same principle holds for the stock market. *Play the odds!* There'll be a bonus for you: the odds of winning are better in the stock market than in any gambling situation. Why is that? Because in a gambling situation, the total payoff, at its maximum, is limited to what the players have kicked in *less* any take for the house. Since there's invariably less in the pot than was initially put in by the players, the chances of winning are less than 50:50, unless a player has some special expertise. That's what is known as a negative-sum game, and that's the reason most gamblers die broke—unless they're really expert. The stock market, on the other hand, is what's known as a positive-sum game. That is, the size of the payoff keeps growing, although irregularly, as long as the economy does. Thus, the chances of making money in the stock market are stacked in your favor.

There's another big drawback in almost any type of gamble. The longer you play in a game where the odds are stacked even *slightly* against you, the more probable becomes your eventual financial demise. But in the investment process, where it's much better than 50:50 that you'll win without effort, your chances for success continue to improve the longer you play. That's why even the simple-minded schemes, the ones that require absolutely no thought, usually turn out to be profitable in the long run (remember the formula plans?). Betting with the odds can turn an essentially unprofitable game like poker into a profitable occupation *if* the betting is done properly. And betting with the odds can turn an essentially profitable game like the stock market into an extremely lucrative venture *when it's done properly.* To do it properly, we need to know *what the odds are.*

Back in Chapter 6, we memorized some numbers that indicated that a typical stock portfolio could be expected to return an average of 10% to 12% per year over the long haul. That was a couple of percentage points per year higher than the blue chip issues that make up the Dow Jones Industrial Average. Of course, the typical stock is a little riskier than are the blue chips, so we'd expect the higher return; it compensates us for accepting the higher risks. To determine what the odds are, we're going to have to use the Dow Jones Industrials as a reference for a while, but keep in mind that the DJIA understates what we really should expect to get by a percent or two a year. I should add that the only reasons for using the Dow Jones Industrial Average as a reference are its historic availability and its widespread popularity.

Since we don't know exactly what's going to happen in the future, our best estimate of the betting odds for stock investment has to be based on what's happened in the past. Not just in the last five years, or ten, but what's happened over a long enough period to cover the big events—the wars, recessions, inflations, assassinations, impeachments, riots, and all the other cataclysms that are likely to recur in our lifetimes. So let's drag out once more that period dating from the final throes of the Great Depression through the first year of Billy Beer—our favorite forty years from 1938 to 1977. And remember, the Dow Jones Industrial Average understates what we can really expect to achieve by at least one or two percent a year.

O.K. Let's say we don't know anything about the odds in the investment game, and we're thinking about buying the Dow Jones Industrials for a period of exactly one year. What can we expect will happen? Based on the average of the last forty years (look back at Table 7-3), we'd probably see a total return of about 9.7% in the next year. Of course, our chances of earning exactly 9.7% are extremely remote. There's a chance we'll lose money, just as there's a chance that we'll make a bundle; the 9.7% figure thus leaves a lot of room for error. Since the market could go either way, the real question is not only, "How much can I expect to make?" but also, "What are the chances that I'll lose?" Again from Table 7-3, the answers are: we can expect to make about 10% (9.7%), and the odds are about 3:1 in our favor—a 73% probability of profit. Not bad betting odds, but can they be improved? The answer to that question is a very definite *yes*.

Remember, we came here looking for a center line for our Variable Ratio plan, and I've already indicated that the appropriate standard is value. We know that the value of stocks in general is determined by the dividend income they generate for us, and the capital gains or losses that occur while we're holding them. Take a look at the graph in Chart 10-1. The stock price series represents the Dow Jones Industrial Average, and the Dividend Yield figures have been computed by dividing the total dividends paid in the preceding four calendar quarters by the DJIA index.

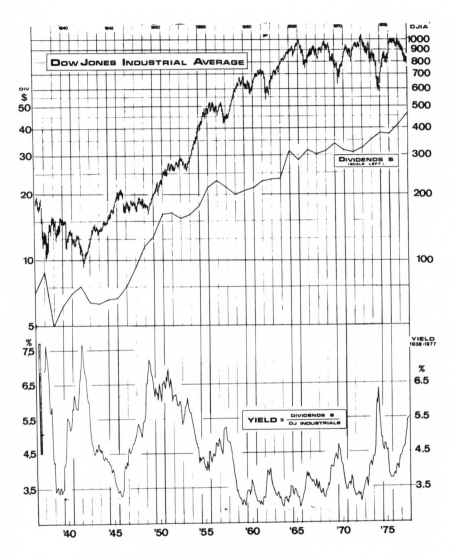

Chart 10-1. Stock prices and dividend yield, 1938–1977.

Notice how the points of *high dividend yield* usually occur at the same time as *major cycle lows* in stock prices. Isn't that neat? High current income and high potential capital gains in one package when the market slips well below its intrinsic value. In other words, bargains! It's obvious that those peaks in the dividend yield series represent times of special opportunity when the odds are heavily biased in our favor. Just how heavily seems to depend on just how undervalued the market becomes. (In this case, normal value—our center line—falls in the $4^1/_4\%$ to $4^1/_2\%$ yield range.) You can see that the strongest price gains come after the market has sold to yield at least $5^1/_2\%$. You can see that prices invariably roar back from the trough levels once the yield gauge has peaked! We'd expect, therefore, to make an excellent return on the dollars we invested when the yield was high. Based on this standard, then, it would seem to make sense for us to bet much more heavily than normal when the market becomes seriously undervalued.

On the other hand, you can see that with the exception of the first half of the 1960s, stocks have never made much progress once they've become overvalued. (It may be worth noting that in 1978 the Dow Jones Industrials sold at the same levels they'd sold at in the early 1960s—nearly two decades with not much progress. The lack of progress, however, doesn't tell the whole story; we'll look into that later.) Yield levels of $3^1/_2\%$ or less should be warning flashers that speculative enthusiasm has gone too far and the market is in real danger of falling apart. Now, when the yields are low, and the betting odds have turned overwhelmingly against us, it makes a lot of sense to ease up on our betting or fold altogether! Sure, we'll miss the ultimate top (and probably have to put up with a few guffaws from our buddies who are playing it to the hilt), but we'll have our stack of chips intact when the game turns our way again.

We've discussed odds in general. Since we've got good market data available to us, we can break them down even more precisely by analyzing the forty-year record. Table 10-1 shows the normal relationship, based on monthly observations of average prices and prevailing dividend yields.

Now that we've got the numbers in front of us, let's try to

Table 10-1. Dividend yield and total one-year return for the Dow Jones Industrial Average, 1938–1977.

Yield Range	Average 1-Year Total Return	Probability of Losing 10% or More	Probability of Gain	Probability of Gaining 5% or More	Probability of Gaining 20% or More
Less than 3.0%	−4.5%	43%	29%	29%	none*
3.01–3.50	0.6	19	50	36	2%
3.51–4.00	8.3	11	77	68	23
4.01–4.50	10.7	10	74	61	32
4.51–5.00	15.7	none*	86	78	33
5.01–5.50	10.8	none*	81	61	23
5.51–6.00	17.0	7	79	64	43
6.01–6.50	16.1	3	89	77	46
6.51–7.00	21.1	none*	100*	100*	54
Over 7.00	33.0	none*	100*	100*	90
Normal	9.7	9	73	46	26

*Observed in period 1938–1977.

figure out what they mean in plain American. First, take a look across the "normal" row at the bottom of the table. That's what you'd expect to get if we didn't know anything at all about the market. It tells you that in a normal year, there's about one chance in ten (9%) that you'd lose more than ten percent on your investment capital. It also tells you that normally you'd expect to make some money about three-quarters (73%) of the time. So the betting odds for a normal year are roughly 3:1 in your favor to begin with, and you could expect to make at least 20% on your investments in one year out of every four. This is important: notice how the odds shift toward you as the yield gets higher, and how they slip away from you as the yield drops. At high yield levels (arbitrarily, over 5½%) the combined odds are better than 4:1 that you'll make at least some money, and it's about 50:50 that you'll make more than 20% on your investment. That's when you ought to be putting more chips on the table. As yields drop, the odds turn from mediocre to poor. At low yield levels, say 3½% or less, it's 3:1 against you that you'll be able to beat the bank, and it's less than 50:50 that you'll get out with all the chips you put into the game. The market would be vulnerable to the first bad-news item that came along, and you wouldn't be getting paid enough to compensate for the risk of losing your shirt.

Like expert poker players, we're now in a position to develop an investment strategy based on known odds. Understand that even betting with the odds doesn't guarantee that every investment you make will turn out to be profitable: it's obviously impossible to win every pot, no matter how strongly the odds are in your favor. But you'll probably have more chips in front of you at the end of the game. Of course, there are thousands of possible tactical combinations we could try. But the most obvious investment strategy is to increase your commitment to the market when it becomes under-valued—when yields are high—and reduce your commitment or get out altogether when it becomes overvalued.

Let's assume you're starting from scratch. You're working with $100 a month to begin your investment program. Let's try a rough set of investing rules that should force you to buy more shares in the fund when prices are low and less—or none at all—when they're high. Here are the figures for a $100-per-month program with investments made quarterly:

If yield is:	Then
Less than 3.5%	Put $100 contribution in cash reserve, nothing into stocks
3.51 to 4.5%	Put $100 contribution into stocks, maintain cash reserve
4.51 to 5.5%	Put $100 contribution and 20% of cash reserve into stocks
Over 5.5%	Put $100 contribution and 50% of cash reserve into stocks

The yield ranges as well as the tactics are somewhat arbitrary, but it's the structure of the rules that's important. These rules force you in the right direction. They keep you buying heavily when everyone else is panicky, they keep you *out* when everyone else is frenzied, and they're easy to adapt to your own particular situation.

Since we've assumed that you're starting from zero, our first objective is to make the cycle work *for* you while you're building capital. At this stage, it's important to see whether you can do any better than you could with simple Dollar Cost Averaging. You remember that Dollar Cost Averaging did a fair job of smoothing out the cycle effects in the first few years, and it allowed you, without much effort, to get in on that long-term trend of 10% to 12% a year. Let's see if a little common sense applied to the problem does any better. In fact, let's compare the results from both Dollar Cost Averaging and the Variable Ratio plan.

We'll need a typical market cycle to work with so we can compare results.

For the sake of simplicity, let's forget about long-term capital gains, dividend income, and any interest you might earn on the dollars you're going to hold in a cash reserve. (Remember, Dollar Cost Averaging never builds a cash reserve, so interest isn't a factor there.) O.K. We've taken out all the elements of return, and we're left with just the cycle. In its cleanest form, the cycle might look something like Chart 10-2, with market prices oscillating around their normal $6 dividend between an upper extreme of 3% (overvalued at around $200) and a lower limit of 6% (undervalued at around $100) with a cycle length of around 4½ years. Obviously, the cycle won't be this regular, but it's fairly typical to find a two- to three-year bull market followed by a one- to two-year bear market. Since we've eliminated all the returns, this wouldn't be much of an investment medium unless we could gain some advantage from the cycle itself. And we can, on the basis of what we now know of cycle limits.

Just for the sake of comparison, let's apply Dollar Cost Averaging to this cycle at $100 a month invested, say, once every quarter for a period of ten years. Table 10-2 shows the results. After ten years, you would have gained a very slight edge ($498) just from the cycle effect. Of course, the basic purpose of any accumulation scheme is to allow you to build up an equity position without the danger of decimation by a single, poorly-timed investment. If the program can do that, and perhaps milk a bit more from the cycle, so much the better.

The workup in Table 10-2 also indicates why so many well-intentioned investment programs end up as failures. (Look, for example, at Year 4, Quarter III and Year 9, Quarter II; how would you feel if these were your dollars?) As we said before,

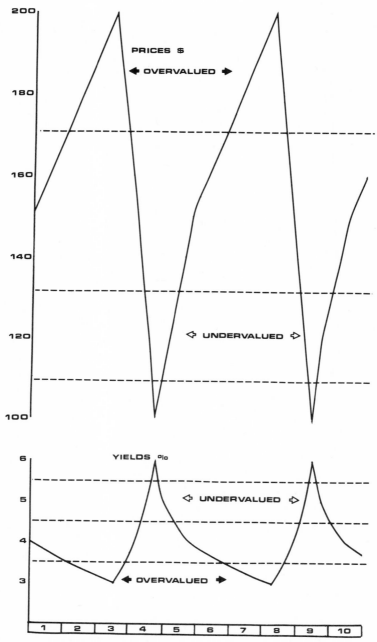

Chart 10-2. Stock prices and dividend yield, typical speculative cycle.

Table 10-2. Dollar Cost Averaging on a quarterly index of 100–200 (cycle effects only).

Year	Quarter	Price Index	Shares in Quarter	Total Shares	Market Value	Invested	Profit or (Loss)
	I	155	1.9	1.9	$ 300	$ 300	—
1	II	160	1.9	3.8	610	600	$ 10
	III	165	1.8	5.6	929	900	29
	IV	170	1.8	7.4	1,257	1,200	57
	I	175	1.7	9.1	1,594	1,500	94
2	II	180	1.7	10.8	1,939	1,800	139
	III	185	1.6	12.4	2,293	2,100	193
	IV	190	1.6	14.0	2,655	2,400	255
	I	195	1.5	15.5	3,025	2,700	325
3	II	200	1.5	17.0	3,403	3,000	403
	III	180	1.7	18.7	3,362	3,300	62
	IV	160	1.9	20.6	3,289	3,600	(311)
	I	140	2.1	22.7	3,178	3,900	(722)
4	II	120	2.5	25.2	3,024	4,200	(1,176)
	III	100	3.0	28.2	2,820	4,500	(1,680)
	IV	120	2.5	30.7	3,684	4,800	(1,116)
	I	130	2.3	33.0	4,291	5,100	(809)
5	II	140	2.1	35.1	4,921	5,400	(479)
	III	150	2.0	37.1	5,572	5,700	(128)
	IV	155	1.9	39.1	6,058	6,000	58
	I	160	1.9	41.0	6,553	6,300	253
6	II	165	1.8	42.8	7,058	6,600	458
	III	170	1.8	44.5	7,572	6,900	672
	IV	175	1.7	46.3	8,095	7,200	895
	I	180	1.7	47.9	8,627	7,500	1,127
7	II	185	1.6	49.5	9,166	7,800	1,366
	III	190	1.6	51.1	9,714	8,100	1,614
	IV	195	1.5	52.7	10,270	8,400	1,870
	I	200	1.5	54.2	10,833	8,700	2,133
8	II	180	1.7	55.8	10,050	9,000	1,050
	III	160	1.9	57.7	9,233	9,300	(67)
	IV	140	2.1	59.8	8,379	9,600	(1,221)
	I	120	2.5	62.3	7,482	9,900	(2,418)
9	II	100	3.0	65.3	6,535	10,200	(3,665)
	III	120	2.5	67.8	8,142	10,500	(2,358)
	IV	130	2.3	70.2	9,120	10,800	(1,680)
	I	140	2.1	72.3	10,122	11,100	(978)
10	II	150	2.0	74.3	11,145	11,400	(255)
	III	155	1.9	76.2	11,816	11,700	116
	IV	160	1.9	78.1	12,498	12,000	498

it's the nature of the human animal to be enthusiastic when things are going well—when he's made a profit—and to feel rotten when things are going poorly—when he's taken a loss. As a result of this psychological quirk, most people celebrate by increasing their commitment as the market approaches its ultimate peak, and by passing or giving up altogether when they're sitting on a fat loss near the market's low! Your gut feel runs exactly counter to what you should be doing; your emotional reactions can defeat the whole purpose of the Dollar Cost Averaging method.

All right, we've decided to play it smarter. We're going to let the normal relationship between market price and true value guide our commitments to the market. When the whole world is panting after common stocks, and it looks as though prices will never stop rising, the dividend yield figures will indicate the speculative overvaluation for us. At that point, we'll play our cards very conservatively, since the odds will be turning against us. On the other hand, when the market looks as though it will never stop falling, dividend yields will rise to abnormally high levels, and we can loosen up our purse strings. Then, when no one else wants them, we'll buy large quantities of stocks with our cash reserve. Again, our strategy will be determined by one element alone—dividend yield. If it's too low—less than $3^{1}/_{2}\%$—we'll put our money into the savings account, since the odds of our making money in the market are about 2:1 *against* us. If yield is in the mid-ranges, the odds become roughly 2:1 in *favor* of our beating the bank, so we'll bet progressively higher amounts as dividend yield increases. When the market becomes grossly undervalued—when yield is over $5^{1}/_{2}\%$—we'll use our cash reserve aggressively to pick up bargains while they're still around. And if the whole world seems to be perched on the edge of some cataclysmic holocaust, with yield over $6^{1}/_{2}\%$, we'll hock the family jewels to buy stocks. If the world really does come to an end, as all the prophets will surely be prophesying, the family jewels won't have been much good for anything anyway! And if it isn't terminal time, our rocks will be a lot bigger a couple of years later.

The question is, does it work? Table 10-3 is the workup on

our no-growth, no-dividends, no-interest cycle. Let's walk through the numbers, since it's important to get a feel for the details of how our system works. The investment action each quarter is determined exclusively by the current yield on the market index. Let's look at quarters I through IV of the first year. Assuming that we begin in mid-cycle, with a dividend payout of $6 a year, prices between $133 and $171 call for normal expenditures to accumulate shares. Next stage: yields fall below the 3¹/₂% warning level early in the second year (2-I) and remain there through the market's peak (3-II). We should be using these quarters to build a cash reserve that will eventually let us make bigger purchases at lower price levels. It's important to notice that at the market's ultimate peak (3-II) less than half of our total capital is exposed to the forthcoming bear market! (Ideally, not one penny of our growing fortune should be exposed to market risks at this juncture. We'll have to make modifications to deal with that problem, but that's for later. Right now, we're busy checking out a yield-based accumulation plan.)

As the market begins its precipitous slide (for a variety of reasons, prices usually fall roughly twice as fast as they rise), yields pass very quickly through the moderate valuations where we continue to add to our market commitment through our regular $300 purchases, in 3-IV and 4-I, and finally into the undervalued areas we've been waiting for. Now we'll begin to bet our cash reserve in addition to the regular amounts. At the 120 price level, in 4-II, yields are sufficiently high to justify using 20% of our cash reserve in addition to the regular $300 contribution. Near the bottom, in 4-III, those abnormally high yields practically scream at us to use half our remaining reserve to pick up absolute steals. So you see that in cycle after cycle, the yield criterion at least points us in the right direction. Now try it yourself. Follow the next cycle in Table 10-3 on your own, to make sure you know the mechanical details of our system. After all, you're the one who's going to use it. Again, I'll remind you that it's not really this clear-cut in the real world. The market has seen a couple of bottoms at yield levels as low as 4%, and on other occasions hasn't stopped dropping until yields reached 7% or higher. So let's

Table 10-3. Modified Dollar Cost Averaging:

Year	Quarter	Price Index	Yield	Action Required
1	I	155	3.87	buy $300
	II	160	3.75	buy 300
	III	165	3.64	buy 300
	IV	170	3.53	buy 300
2	I	175	3.43	$300 to cash
	II	180	3.33	300 to cash
	III	185	3.24	300 to cash
	IV	190	3.16	300 to cash
3	I	195	3.08	$300 to cash
	II	200	3.00	300 to cash
	III	180	3.33	300 to cash
	IV	160	3.75	buy $300
4	I	140	4.29	buy $300
	II	120	5.00	buy 300 + $420 = $ 720
	III	100	6.00	buy 300 + 840 = 1,140
	IV	120	5.00	buy 300 + 168 = 468
5	I	130	4.62	buy $300 + $134 = $ 434
	II	140	4.29	buy 300
	III	150	4.00	buy 300
	IV	155	3.87	buy 300
6	I	160	3.75	buy $300
	II	165	3.64	buy 300
	III	170	3.53	buy 300
	IV	175	3.43	$300 to cash
7	I	180	3.33	$300 to cash
	II	185	3.24	300 to cash
	III	190	3.16	300 to cash
	IV	195	3.08	300 to cash
8	I	200	3.00	$300 to cash
	II	180	3.33	300 to cash
	III	160	3.75	buy $300
	IV	140	4.29	buy 300
9	I	120	5.00	buy $300 + $ 528 = $ 828
	II	100	6.00	buy 300 + 1,055 = 1,355
	III	120	5.00	buy 300 + 211 = 511
	IV	130	4.62	buy 300 + 169 = 469
10	I	140	4.29	buy $300
	II	150	4.00	buy 300
	III	155	3.87	buy 300
	IV	160	3.75	buy 300

yield-based with cash reserve.

Shares This Quarter	Total Shares	Market Value	To Cash	Total Cash	Total Value	Profit or (Loss)
1.9	1.9	$ 300	—		$ 300	—
1.9	3.8	610	—		610	$ 10
1.8	5.6	929	—		929	29
1.8	7.4	1,257	—		1,257	57
—	7.4	1,294	$ 300	$ 300	1,594	94
—	7.4	1,331	300	600	1,931	131
—	7.4	1,368	300	900	2,268	168
—	7.4	1,405	300	1,200	2,605	205
—	7.4	1,442	300	1,500	2,942	242
—	7.4	1,479	300	1,800	3,279	279
—	7.4	1,331	300	2,100	3,431	131
1.9	9.3	1,483	—	2,100	3,583	(17)
2.1	11.4	1,598	—	2,100	3,698	(202)
6.0	17.4	2,089	−420	1,680	3,769	(431)
11.4	28.8	2,881	−840	840	3,721	(779)
3.9	32.7	3,925	−168	672	4,597	(203)
3.3	36.0	4,687	−134	538	5,225	125
2.1	38.2	5,347	—	538	5,885	485
2.0	40.2	6,029	—	538	6,567	867
1.9	42.1	6,530	—	538	7,068	1,068
1.9	44.0	7,041	—	538	7,579	1,279
1.8	45.8	7,561	—	538	8,099	1,499
1.8	47.6	8,090	—	538	8,628	1,728
—	47.6	8,328	300	838	9,166	1,966
—	47.6	8,565	300	1,138	9,703	2,203
—	47.6	8,803	300	1,438	10,241	2,441
—	47.6	9,041	300	1,738	10,779	2,679
—	47.6	9,279	300	2,038	11,317	2,917
—	47.6	9,517	300	2,338	11,855	3,155
—	47.6	8,565	300	2,638	11,203	2,203
1.9	49.5	7,914	—	2,638	10,552	1,252
2.1	51.6	7,224	—	2,638	9,862	262
6.9	58.5	7,020	−528	2,110	9,130	(770)
13.6	72.1	7,205	−1,055	1,055	8,260	(1,940)
4.3	76.3	9,157	−211	844	10,001	(499)
3.6	79.9	10,389	−169	675	11,064	264
2.1	82.1	11,489	—	675	12,164	1,064
2.0	84.1	12,609	—	675	13,284	1,884
1.9	86.0	13,329	—	675	14,004	2,304
1.9	87.9	14,059	—	675	14,734	2,734

understand that we're not talking about precision timing—just betting with *the odds!*

The payoff of this simple plan is shown on the bottom line in the right-hand column of Table 10-3. No growth, no dividends, no interest earned on our sometimes substantial cash position, and yet we made a few bucks—$2734, to be exact—just from playing the cycle. Nothing to write home about, perhaps, but quite a lot more than Dollar Cost Averaging could have given us, because we were constantly *betting with the odds!* (Just compare the results in Table 10-2 with those in Table 10-3!) As important as the *amount* of money we made is the fact that we *rarely held a serious loss position.* Since we built a cash reserve early, and the money in it was immune to market risks, our overall profit or loss position was usually much better under this yield-based scheme than it was under straight Dollar Cost Averaging. Psychologically, that made it a lot easier to stick with the plan. And our cash reserve allowed us to pick up some real bargains when nobody else wanted them.

"Wait a minute," you're saying. "If we were constantly betting with the odds, how come we had almost ten thousand bucks in that sucker when the market peaked at the start of the eighth year? That was about 80% of our marbles on the line when we should have folded. *I* was smart enough to figure out that the betting odds weren't too good at that point; how come the plan didn't show it up?"

That's a problem. I said a minute ago that we'd have to do something about that and we will. But before we go tinkering, let's take a hard look at what we've got so far, particularly on the buying side. The structure we've built at least keeps us from buying *anything* when the market is wildly overvalued, and it forces us to step up our buying as the market becomes more and more undervalued. We aren't going to hit the exact trough with one spectacular purchase, but we aren't going to be stuck with a block of Levitz at $240 a share either. So while it's not a complete scheme yet, it's half of a halfway decent method for getting money and keeping it. Once it's completed, we'll put the whole thing to the test against as lousy a market as you could ask for, 1968 to 1977, and we'll see how it would have worked. Or if you don't care about the details, you can check Chapter 12 right now.

All right. You put your finger on a problem. And the problem is that we're leaving ourselves exposed to the bite of the bear when we should be getting a lot more defensive as the market moves into overvalued territory. Once the yield sinks below $3^1/2\%$ or so, the odds of making any money fade fast, and the odds of making a bunch of money are close to nil. There comes a time when it's a whole lot smarter not to play the game at all than it is to stick around for the thrill of making another few bucks.

So let's be smart enough to duck when we know the hurts are coming. When we see that the market's gone too far above what it's really worth, let's stand back and leave to someone else the honor of playing the greatest fool. It's easy enough to incorporate into our plan a selling routine based on dividend yield, just as we used the yield gauge to guide our buying. Again, let me emphasize that we're not talking about real-world expected results yet. What we're attempting to do is develop a structure we expect will fit the real world of the future. To do that, we'll look at past relationships and use them to compare alternate schemes. We've already made one big improvement over the traditional Dollar Cost Averaging method simply by incorporating a cash reserve and using it to buy much more heavily near major cycle lows. Now we're ready to improve on that method by building the size of the cash reserve more rapidly through a progressive selling routine as we approach the vicinity of major market peaks.

Since it's all based on historic dividend/price relationships, maybe we'd better check back to Chart 10-1 and Table 10-1 to see just how realistic our guides are. Chart 10-1 shows us that the market frequently reaches its final peak at yields below $3^1/2\%$, which is when we consider it dangerously overvalued. And as you can see from the experience of the 1960s and the early 1970s, the market can stay in an overvalued area without suffering a major collapse for considerable periods of time. Suppose we'd played it safe and not bought during those go-go days. We'd probably have looked silly by the time of that

1968 high. But 1969–1970 and 1973–1974 left a lot of the party-goers with a pretty rough hangover, because they kept thinking things would go higher still. So we're probably wise to take a slower approach to selling than we took to buying. On the other hand, if we study the odds listed in Table 10-1, we'll see that there's virtually no chance of making a killing when the market is overvalued. In other words, we should walk quickly toward, rather than run for, the safety of our exit—our cash reserve—as yields slump below $3^1/2\%$.

As with our earlier examples, we'll be making the restrictive assumption that stocks yield absolutely no income—no secular growth, no dividend receipt or reinvestment, no interest earned on our substantial cash holdings. If we realize any profit from our method, it's simply because we've captured the cyclic price fluctuations brought about by changes in speculative demand. And those changes are what we're trying to measure with the yield yardstick. We'll maintain our earlier modified buying rules when the market is undervalued, and we'll incorpoarate a slow but progressive selling program in the overvalued area. Again, figures are for a $100-per-month program with investments made quarterly.

If yield is:	Then
Less than 3.5%	Put $100 into cash reserve and sell 20% of stocks held
3.51 to 4.5%	Put $100 into stocks, sell nothing, maintain cash reserve
4.51 to 5.5%	Put $100 and 20% of cash reserve into stocks
Over 5.5%	Put $100 and 50% of cash reserve into stocks

Again, the yield ranges and the particular tactics are arbitrary. There are countless combinations we could try, but it's the structure and not the detail that's important at this point. Now the rules are forcing us to withdraw from the game as the odds turn against us, so that we sell into an overvalued market, and to become increasingly committed as the odds turn progressively better, so that we use our cash reserve more aggressively in an undervalued market.

Table 10-4 is the workup for our modified Variable Ratio plan. Notice that the percentage of our total wealth committed to the market rises when prices fall and declines as the market advances. Just as we did with earlier tables, we'll have to walk through Table 10-4 to help you understand all the shuffling of numbers between stocks and cash. Imagine what it would be like if we'd included dividend receipts and interest earnings!

Don't look at the payoff in the bottom right-hand corner because I don't want you to get so excited you can't crunch through the details. All right, now that you've sneaked a peek, let's get down to work and see how it's done.

It's the same cycle as before, and you get the same results through the first four quarters, as you noted in Tables 10-2 and 10-3; take a minute to check back and compare. Not too dynamic, right? But starting with 2-I, your tactics change. Now you begin bailing out as you see danger coming. Going into 2-I, you've got 7.4 shares and no cash. At an index value of 175 and a yield of 3.43% on the $6 dividend, the market is becoming overvalued, so you'll sell off 20% of your holdings $(0.2 \times 7.3934$ shares held $= 1.4787$ shares sold at $175 = $258.77 proceeds, with 5.9147 shares retained at $175 = $1035.07 market value of shares retained) to generate $259 in cash. Add the normal $300 cash contribution and you've got a safe kitty of $559 in cash, with $1035 still exposed to the market; your total wealth at this point is $559 + $1035 = $1594. At 2-I, you're holding a profit position of $94. Same story in each of the next six quarters, as the market remains overvalued. You continue to sell off one-fifth of your remaining shares, leaving fewer and fewer as time goes on, and you sock the proceeds, along with the regular $300 contribution, into your cash reserve. You're slowly—but not too slowly—decreasing the share of your assets that would be in danger if there were an outright crash. The selling you did here as the market rose to the overvalued level built up a much larger cash reserve near the ultimate peak than you held under the no-selling program. This larger cash reserve will enable you—and the plan rules will *force* you—to be a much more aggressive buyer near the next cyclic low. Lookin' good! That's exactly what we had in mind.

As the market slides past its speculative high, in 3-IV and 4-I, you'll switch from selling to light buying, and then you'll begin using your cash reserve through the final trough.

Table 10-4. Modified plan:

Year	Quarter	Price Index	Yield		Action
1	I	155	3.87	buy	$300
	II	160	3.75	buy	300
	III	165	3.64	buy	300
	IV	170	3.53	buy	300
2	I	175	3.43	sell	$259 + $300 to cash
	II	180	3.33	sell	213 + 300 to cash
	III	185	3.24	sell	175 + 300 to cash
	IV	190	3.16	sell	144 + 300 to cash
3	I	195	3.08	sell	$118 + $300 to cash
	II	200	3.00	sell	97 + 300 to cash
	III	180	3.33	sell	70 + 300 to cash
	IV	160	3.75	buy	300
4	I	140	4.29	buy	$300
	II	120	5.00	buy	300 + $ 635 from cash
	III	100	6.00	buy	300 + 1,271 from cash
	IV	120	5.00	buy	300 + 254 from cash
5	I	130	4.62	buy	$300 + $ 203 from cash
	II	140	4.29	buy	300
	III	150	4.00	buy	300
	IV	155	3.87	buy	300
6	I	160	3.75	buy	$ 300
	II	165	3.64	buy	300
	III	170	3.53	buy	300
	IV	175	3.43	sell	1,718 + $300 to cash
7	I	180	3.33	sell	$1,414 + $300 to cash
	II	185	3.24	sell	1,162 + 300 to cash
	III	190	3.16	sell	955 + 300 to cash
	IV	195	3.08	sell	784 + 300 to cash
8	I	200	3.00	sell	$643 + $300 to cash
	II	180	3.33	sell	463 + 300 to cash
	III	160	3.75	buy	300
	IV	140	4.29	buy	300
9	I	120	5.00	buy	$300 + $2,010 from cash
	II	100	6.00	buy	300 + 4,021 from cash
	III	120	5.00	buy	300 + 804 from cash
	IV	130	4.62	buy	300 + 643 from cash
10	I	140	4.29	buy	$300
	II	150	4.00	buy	300
	III	155	3.87	buy	300
	IV	160	3.75	buy	300

20% of stock holdings sold each quarter.

Shares This Quarter	Total Shares	Market Value	To Cash	From Cash	Total Cash	Total Value	Profit or (Loss)
1.9	1.9	$ 300	—	—	—	$ 300	—
1.9	3.8	610	—	—	—	610	$ 10
1.8	5.6	929	—	—	—	929	29
1.8	7.4	1,257	—	—	—	1,257	57
−1.5	5.9	1,035	$ 559	—	$ 559	1,594	94
−1.2	4.7	852	513	—	1,072	1,924	124
−0.9	3.8	700	475	—	1,547	2,247	147
−0.8	3.0	575	444	—	1,991	2,566	166
−0.6	2.4	473	418	—	2,409	2,882	182
−0.5	1.9	388	397	—	2,806	3,194	194
−0.4	1.6	279	370	—	3,176	3,455	155
1.9	3.4	548	—	—	3,176	3,724	124
2.1	5.6	780	—	—	3,176	3,956	56
7.8	13.4	1,603	—	$−635	2,541	4,144	(56)
15.7	29.1	2,907	—	−1,271	1,270	4,177	(323)
4.6	33.7	4,042	—	−254	1,016	5,058	258
3.9	37.6	4,882	—	−203	813	5,695	595
2.1	39.7	5,558	—	—	813	6,371	971
2.0	41.1	6,255	—	—	813	7,068	1,368
1.9	43.6	6,764	—	—	813	7,577	1,577
1.9	45.5	7,281	—	—	813	8,094	1,794
1.8	47.3	7,809	—	—	813	8,622	2,022
1.8	49.1	8,345	—	—	813	9,158	2,258
−9.8	39.3	6,872	2,018	—	2,831	9,703	2,503
−7.9	31.4	5,655	1,714	—	4,545	10,200	2,700
−6.3	25.1	4,650	1,462	—	6,007	10,657	2,857
−5.0	20.1	3,820	1,255	—	7,262	11,082	2,982
−4.0	16.1	3,137	1,084	—	8,346	11,483	3,083
−3.2	12.9	2,574	943	—	9,289	11,863	3,163
−2.6	10.3	1,853	763	—	10,052	11,905	2,905
1.9	12.2	1,947	—	—	10,052	11,999	2,699
2.1	14.3	2,004	—	—	10,052	12,056	2,456
19.3	33.6	4,028	—	−2,010	8,042	12,070	2,170
43.2	76.8	7,677	—	−4,021	4,021	11,698	1,498
9.2	86.0	10,317	—	−804	3,217	13,534	3,034
7.3	93.2	12,119	—	−643	2,574	14,693	3,893
2.1	95.4	13,352	—	—	2,574	15,926	4,826
2.0	97.4	14,605	—	—	2,574	17,179	5,779
1.9	99.3	15,392	—	—	2,574	17,966	6,266
1.9	101.2	16,189	—	—	2,574	18,763	6,763

You've got a ton of cash in the middle of a recession (or depression) *when it counts the most!* You're using your reserve just as you did in the previous scheme, except that your early sales have given you a much larger reserve to work with. Compare the dollar amounts and the number of shares bought near the cycle lows under this plan with Table 10-2 or Table 10-3. *Now you're really using the cycle to your advantage.* And the final results of your profit and loss position ($6763 profit from a nowhere cycle) clearly indicate that the principle behind Variable Ratio—selling into overvalued markets, buying into undervalued—is forcing you in the right direction at all times. Sure, you're going to miss the extremes; you'll never dump your entire holdings at the highest possible price and you'll never take on a full load on the very day of the bottom—but you won't miss them by too wide a margin.

We can appreciate the common-sense features of this scheme because by now we've got some understanding of historic speculative cycles, we understand the odds, and unlike the crowd, we're betting with the odds, not against them. One of the best features of the scheme is that the profit or loss scene is easy to accept. Since we're taking defensive moves to protect ourselves when prices get out of touch with economic reality, our chances of sitting on a substantial losing position are greatly reduced. Personally, I wouldn't have the guts to plunk down another hundred or thousand bucks if I were already holding a 30% or 40% loser, so I'd make a lousy Dollar Cost Averager. It would just make me sick to watch my money vanish into thin air. And I'd take damn small consolation from knowing that my $300 could buy three full shares instead of only one and a half, if I'd already accumulated a hundred shares over the years. Defense, on the other hand, I can live with. And this system forces us to get defensive when the odds turn sour!

At the risk of sounding redundant, let me emphasize once more that what we should be looking at in this section is the structure, not the details, of the modified Variable Ratio plan. I'm a firm believer that life has about twenty universal laws, including the ten in stone and Murphy's. Murphy's Law, which says "If anything can go wrong, it will," seems the most pervasive. So it's only fair to approach any investment program with a premonition that the details will have to be modified to account for future changes in our definitions of "undervalued" or "overvalued." But on the basis of the odds as we've measured them over the last forty years, the plan's structure seems sound and its yield gauge seems workable. As I promised you, we'll get to a full-blown simulation of this method over one of the rottenest decades in market history. We'll see that it performed like a champ even then; that may convince us that it's worth a try. To the extent that the 1980s and 1990s are similar to the 1940s, 1950s, 1960s, and 1970s, we'd have a right to expect similar results. To the extent that future decades differ, we'll do somewhat better or worse. But we've got one more detail to clean up first.

Pick a Fund
That Swings

WE'VE got a method for taking advantage of the recurring speculative cycles—our Variable Ratio. The only remaining requirement is a specific investment vehicle to do the job for us. In simple terms, we need a place to send our monthly check. We've seen that a no-load mutual fund is the only really smart way to get started in the investment process. But there are over 150 of them out there, so how do we know which individual fund will suit our needs? That's what we'll be up to in this chapter—picking one or a few no-load funds that best meet the requirements of high growth and high volatility. Then, once we've narrowed the field, we can combine our aggressive no-load vehicle with our Variable Ratio method into a complete system and test it against actual market data. If it works (and after ten chapters, it had better work), it should give us a very clear idea of what we can expect in the future.

Before we jump into the fund selection process, let's review our reasons for using a mutual fund in the first place. Obviously, if you think you can pick the high flyer of the 1980s, it would be silly not to put all your eggs in that basket. But if past track records are any guide to future expectations, virtually no one has the knack for knowing in advance which individual stock is going to be next year's big winner—or, for that matter, big loser. No one—not the mutual fund manager, not the bank trust officer, not the nationally advertised investment adviser, not the broker—*no one* has been consistently able to pick the winners and avoid the losers. And I don't have to tell you there are a lot of smart people working full-time on the "which stock?" problem. They're armed with computers and advanced degrees and they've been trying for a century. But no one's really got a handle on it yet. The implication is that if *they* can't do it with all the resources at their disposal, you probably aren't going to be able to take the local newspaper and your six-function calculator and come up with the answer either. Therein lies the most compelling reason for using a no-load mutual fund instead of an individual stock: safety in numbers, diversification—and at no initial cost.

Diversification simply means that we're not betting all our money on one horse. It assures us that we won't get stuck holding onto a loser while the rest of the market is chugging upward. It may also mean that we won't be holding a winner when the general trend of prices is down, but our Variable Ratio plan should help on that account. Diversification means that we'll get the market—nothing more, nothing less. We'll miss the thrill of riding all the way up on Houston Oil & Minerals, which went from under 25¢ a share in 1970 to over $42 by 1977, but neither will we get trapped in an Ampex, which dropped from nearly $50 a share in 1969 to $2 a share in 1974. Diversification provides us with protection against the potential devastation of a complete financial wipe-out; it costs us whatever slim chance we might have had for hitting a one-shot jackpot.

And diversification is exactly what we get in a mutual fund. Most funds hold from thirty to as many as several hundred individual stocks—not necessarily superior stocks, just lots of them. Since the funds hold so many stocks, their atrocious picks are approximately canceled out by the ones they brag about, and their net investment performance tends to parallel that of the broad market. By selecting stocks for us, the funds save us a needless waste of time and energy, and allow us to concentrate on more important matters like "Where's the market going?" and "How much of my money is exposed?" That's enough to have to worry about!

The second advantage of no-load funds is that they save us money we might otherwise have to spend on commissions because we buy our shares directly from the fund at their true net asset value. The 8³/₄% the load funds demand is a big slice in anybody's book, especially since load funds don't do any better than no-loads. And the 1% or 2% to the broker may not seem like any big deal, but if you don't have to give money away, why do it?

Diversification, an essential! And no commissions, a bonus. What else? Think back to our discussions on the various formula plans. With any of those formulas, high volatility usually produced higher profit positions. Simply because it goes up a lot faster in the bullish phase and falls a lot faster in the bearish phase—because it magnifies the cycle effect—a highly volatile vehicle produces significantly better investment results. And now that we have an imperfect but workable method for at least partially avoiding the bear market phase, *high volatility is an absolute must.* If our Variable Ratio method is any good at all, we should be able to ride a screamer up. After we take a graceful exit near the top, who cares how fast it falls?

It's comparatively easy to determine how fast a mutual fund will move on any specified change in the market index. It's a much more difficult process to predict how an individual stock will behave in a bull or bear market. While virtually all mutual funds go up in a bullish phase and down in a bearish phase, lots of individual stocks just don't conform to the broad market's trend. The reason is that there are so many factors unique to an individual company—its own earnings, dividends, growth rates, financial status, speculative appeal, investor interest, good-news or bad-news surprises—all of these can influence its price. For any single stock, the broad market's direction is just one of those factors. In recent years, the Beta statistic has arisen as the investment community's partial answer to the "what to expect from this stock" problem, and the measure is of some value in determining how volatile a stock might be. But compared to the relatively high degree of accuracy with which we can measure a mutual fund's rate of response to market changes, using the Beta statistic to measure a stock's future response is rather crude. And fortunately, it's unnecessary.

I'll tell you why. The volatility of a mutual fund is pretty much determined by its stated investment objectives—growth, income, balanced or special-purpose—and by the market sector in which the portfolio manager concentrates. For example, we wouldn't expect too much price action either way in a fund that holds high-grade bonds or low-risk stocks. So they're not what we need. On the other hand, a fund that concentrates its portfolio in emerging stocks traded on the American Stock Exchange, or in the over-the-counter market, could soar like an eagle in the right market environment. And it would probably have a stronger secular uptrend than the blue-chip sector, simply because many AMEX and OTC stocks will probably be household names in the 1980s and 1990s. So it comes down to this. If we want a screamer to put our chips on in a bull market, we'll be looking for an aggressive, capital-gains-oriented, no-load fund that concentrates its own portfolio in smaller growth stocks. It's likely to get crushed in a bear market, of course, so we'll have to rely on our Variable Ratio scheme to get us out of it before it collapses.

The final important advantage of no-load mutual funds over individual stocks arises from what is known as a *switch arrangement,* a special arrangement many of the funds maintain with money-market funds. "What's a money-market fund?" One of the *special purpose* no-load funds. This kind of fund invests exclusively in money-market instruments like commercial paper, certificates of deposit, and treasury bills. "Well, that doesn't sound too dynamic." It isn't dynamic—but it's safe! It's a safe place to store our idle cash (remember, we're going to have a pretty fair-sized hunk of change lying around in our cash reserve from time to time). It's a good way to earn daily interest often at higher rates than those available at the bank, and you can switch cash into or out of your no-load stock fund simply by calling a toll-free telephone number. In other words, you can purchase or redeem shares in the fund and have the cash reserve earning more cash every day with an absolute minimum of effort on your part. Add them up: daily interest plus no-hassle toll-free telephone purchases and redemptions; throw in a check-writing privilege, IRA and Keogh plans if you want them, and monthly reports on your cash balance with its interest accrued, and you've got an extremely safe, highly liquid switch arrangement for your investment account. The switch idea is only a couple of years old and it's caught on like wildfire. Within a few years, dozens of funds will have the switching feature.

We're looking for an aggressive no-load mutual fund that concentrates on capital gains, is diversified chiefly into smaller growth companies, and—most importantly—has high volatility. We'd like to be able to set up a Keogh or IRA plan so we can shelter our money from the taxman legally. And we'd like a modest minimum initial purchase requirement so we can get started on a few hundred bucks. If it has a switch arrangement with a money-market fund, so much the better. First, though, we need a screamer. Where are we going to find this little beastie?

I suggested the best source of information on no-load funds back in Chapter 7, when I asked you to write the No-Load Mutual Fund Association. (There are advisory services that follow the no-load funds; they'll sell you their analyses for a fee, but you can do just as good a job of finding the best funds on your own.) Now that you've got the Association's brochure, which lists virtually every no-load registered in the country, the time has come for a little homework. You'll need performance numbers—*Barron's* does an excellent recap of mutual fund performance and it should also be your primary guide as you set up and follow through on your investment program. I suggest you get a subscription right now to this weekly gold mine of ideas. It's all you'll need.

O.K. now. Spread out the NLMFA membership directory

along with the addendum, which lists the newest registrants, and let's do a little culling. To begin with, forget about the "Growth and Income," "Income," and "Money Market" classifications—we need volatility first and foremost. Then scratch out all those funds with over about $100 million in total assets. They're too large to be able to move into and out of the dynamic, fast-growth sector of the market without causing a huge wave. The smaller funds can establish significant positions, relative to their size, in potential movers without much of a ripple, but the biggies have to play General Motors and AT&T, and those aren't the sort of stocks we have in mind. Now we're down to somewhere between thirty and fifty funds. Let's cut it some more by checking each fund to see if we can afford to get into it. What is its minimum purchase requirement? I don't know exactly what you're starting with, but for my money a thousand bucks is just about tops for the initial capital I'm putting into any single fund. As a practical matter, we'll end up holding three or four funds, so do whatever you can afford. Next, sight down the columns labeled "Objective" and "Investment Policy," and look for words like "maximum capital gains," "smaller growth companies," "potential appreciation," "leverage," or anything else that might indicate that the fund could be a swinger.

Now you're down to ten or twenty semifinal candidates. At this point, you'll need to truck over to the public library for a while. But before you head out the door, check the remaining funds for a listing in *Barron's* Mutual Fund section. If you can't find them there, they're probably too new, with too few assets to be listed. That doesn't mean they're not good; it just means they probably have less than $5 million under management. One thing that will happen to you after you've put a few hundred, or maybe a thousand, bucks on the line is that you'll become increasingly interested in how your fund is doing. If the fund isn't listed in the financial press, how are you going to know?

All right. Off to the library for a copy of *Investment Companies* by Wiesenberger. Look up each of the ten or twenty funds left on your list and write down their performance records for, say, the last five or six years, as I've done in Table 11-1.

Table 11-1. Percent annual change no-load funds and NYSE Composite Index.

	1972		1973		1974		1975		1976		1977	
Fund												
A	31	1*	−46	5	−47	3	77	2	22	4	18	1
B	−5	5	−36	3	−50	4	184	1	46	2	9	3
C	−10	6	−53	6	−58	6	16	6	43	3	5	4
.			.		.		.		.		.	
.			.		.		.		.		.	
.			.		.		.		.		.	
X	12	3	−21	2	−22	1	30	3	64	1	16	2
Y	9	4	−40	4	−55	5	17	5	21	5	3	5
Z	20	2	−1	1	−25	2	20	4	20	6	−4	6
NYSE Index	14.3%		−19.6%		−30.3%		31.9%		21.5%		−9.3%	

*Boldface figures show rankings of funds for years indicated.

This will give you a rough idea of which funds you'll want to look into further. Then rank the funds for each year's performance from best to worst (1 to 6 on my chart). As you go over the results of this tabulation, it'll become obvious that some funds never do as well as others. For example, compare the performance of fund B with that of fund C. In bear market years, fund C always loses more than fund B; in bull market years, it always gains less. Why in the world would you want to own C when you could get B? You wouldn't! In the trade, C is known as a *dominated* investment (an academic term for "not so hot"), and a careful examination of your list of twenty will probably reveal several other dominate/subordinate relationships between the various funds. And you know what we'll do with those subordinates—kick 'em out! Kick out Y. Why? Compare X and Y. X always does better than Y, that's why. The appropriate question to ask is this: *Does any one fund do consistently better than any other fund?* Simply keep matching your rank numbers and you should be able to pare the list down to a minimum of five and a maximum of ten or twelve finalists. Incidentally, you'll notice that, as a general rule, the funds that really crashed hard in 1973 and 1974 were the real winners when the market finally turned up! Since we hope to drop out of the game during bear markets and avoid most of the damage, we're most interested in those funds that have proven they can fly when it's time for a bull market. Anyway, we're down to less than a dozen likely candidates, and now we need to write to each for a prospectus.

Writing for the prospectus is a simple enough matter; a postcard with "Please send a current prospectus and most recent statements to" will do the trick. But it takes a lawyer to interpret the prospectus once you get it. Check the fund's objectives and investment policies to make sure its sights are on maximum capital gains, then look pretty carefully over the latest annual reports to the shareholders. Included will be a listing of the securities in the fund's portfolio. This is a tipoff to its expected volatility. If the portfolio consists of issuers that are already household names (IBM and Exxon, for instance) it won't move much faster than the market, nor can you expect it to grow much faster over the long term than will the overall economy. Instead, we're looking for emerging growth companies. They'll swing faster than the general market and, if history is any guide, they'll be the fastest-growing segment of the economy. If there are a bunch of names you don't recognize, don't worry. By the time they're familiar to everyone, they will already have experienced almost all of their really dynamic growth.

One more library assignment and then we'll be able to pick the three or four funds that are best suited to our Variable Ratio plan. I recommend that you use three or four funds for one primary reason: no one can predict precisely which fund will do best in a future bull market, but we can reasonably expect three former leaders to move up very strongly; if there's been a significant change in the investment policy of one of them, you're covered by the other two. Using three or four funds in roughly equal proportion assures us that we'll get the upside velocity we're looking for.

Back to the library with one last worksheet to select our no-load fund portfolio. This time, we're going to repeat the process of evaluating volatility with respect to the market, but now that we're down to less than a dozen funds, we'll give each one the detailed attention it deserves. We need to know just how fast we can expect these funds to move on major rallies and declines in the broad market, so we can understand just how

Table 11-2. Major rallies, NYSE Composite Index 1972–1977.

	1/7/72– 1/5/73	7/6/73– 10/12/73	10/4/74– 11/18/74	12/6/74– 7/11/75	9/12/75– 12/31/76	Average Change Over All 5 Periods
NYSE Index	57.20– 65.37	53.36– 60.25	32.90– 39.63	34.45– 50.71	44.26– 57.88	
% Change	14.3	12.9	20.5	47.2	30.8	25.1
L	18.6	15.9	32.6	122.6	45.7	47.1
M	39.1	17.1	19.5	94.5	48.6	43.8
N	80.9	49.0	31.1	153.4	67.6	76.4
.	.	.	.	.	.	.
.	.	.	.	.	.	.
.	.	.	.	.	.	.
R	53.0	4.1	16.4	40.1	99.3	42.6
S	30.4	36.5	55.4	54.5	81.2	51.6

potentially profitable—or potentially awful—they will be. Table 11-2 lists every major rally on the NYSE Composite Index over the six years from 1972 through 1977, using an arbitrary minimum change of +10%. It'll allow us to compare the funds' gains after we've filled in the blanks.

To fill in the blanks, we'll need to refer to back issues of *Barron's,* which most libraries keep in bound volumes. (For the sake of simplicity, we're going to ignore any distributions the funds may have paid out, but that won't materially affect the volatility measures for these funds.) Table 11-2 shows week-endings, so we can go directly to the Mutual Fund section of *Barron's* (issue date is the Monday following) and record the price of each of our finalists on those eleven closings, as in Table 11-3.

Then convert the raw price changes to percentage changes and enter the gains for each fund in a format similar to Table 11-2. And just to get an indication of how much it can hurt when Murphy's Law strikes in full fury, list the losses as I have here in Table 11-4.

The whole purpose of this exercise, of course, is to find a select group of three or four no-loads that really *move* when the market rallies. As a result of our efforts, we should be able to isolate several funds that will rise two or three times as fast as the NYSE Index with a pretty high degree of consistency.

Table 11-3. Weekly closing prices of selected funds for key dates, 1972–1977.

NYSE Index	1/7/72	1/5/73	7/6/73	10/12/73	10/4/74	11/18/74	12/6/74	7/11/75	9/12/75	12/31/76	11/4/77
	57.20	65.37	53.36	60.25	32.90	39.63	34.45	50.71	44.26	57.88	49.78
L	14.92	17.70	12.21	14.15	5.58	7.40	5.01	11.15	9.62	14.02	16.07
M	10.15	14.12	11.18	13.09	7.71	9.21	7.04	13.69	12.91	19.18	18.35
N	5.91	10.69	8.13	12.11	4.92	6.45	4.40	11.15	9.68	16.22	13.09
. . .											
R	19.16	29.32	18.41	19.16	12.19	14.19	10.79	15.12	14.89	29.68	26.12
S	10.02	13.07	11.73	16.01	7.81	12.14	8.36	12.92	12.15	22.02	16.09

Table 11-4. Major declines in the NYSE Composite Index 1972–1977.

NYSE Index	1/5/73– 7/6/73	10/12/73– 10/4/74	11/18/74– 12/6/74	7/11/75– 9/12/75	12/31/76– 11/4/77	Average Change Over All 5 Periods
% Change	65.37 to 53.36	60.25 to 32.90	39.63 to 34.45	50.71 to 44.26	57.88 to 49.78	
	–18.4	–45.4	–13.1	–12.7	–14.0	–20.7
L	–31.0	–60.6	–32.3	–13.7	14.6	–24.6
M	–20.8	–41.1	–23.6	–5.7	–4.3	–19.1
N	–23.9	–59.4	–31.8	–13.2	–19.3	–29.5
. . .						
R	–37.2	–36.4	–24.0	–1.5	–12.0	–22.2
S	–10.3	–51.2	–31.1	–6.0	–26.9	–25.1

Unfortunately, they'll also fall one-and-a-half to two times as fast as the market does when it decides to turn south, but we trust that our modified Variable Ratio plan is going to protect us from that.

For the final selection, let's pick a package of the three highest upside volatility funds that are registered for sale in our state and that have a minimum initial purchase requirement of $1000 or less. Looking over our tables, we'd choose fund N, which usually moves up 3.0 times as fast as the general market; fund S, which rises 2.1 times as fast; and fund L (1.9 times as fast). If we put equal dollar amounts into each of the three funds, we'd expect an overall portfolio gain that better than doubles that of the market ($0.333 \times 3.0 + 0.333 \times 2.1 + 0.333 \times 1.9 = 2.3$) during the bullish cycle. If we wanted even more volatility (but let me warn you, that's being a little greedy; it's awfully risky), we could increase our invested capital in fund N and cut back on our commitment to L. And notice from the 1973–1974 experience that these funds aren't the place to be when the market's falling apart.

So what have we got with all our charts and tables and figures? So far, we've got the modified Variable Ratio plan to get us aggressively into the market when it's grossly undervalued (usually, you remember, near a major low in prices) and to take us out in a series of defensive steps when it becomes overvalued near the ultimate peak in prices. We know that we'll never hit it precisely at either turning point, so we're planning to make our profits out of the *middle* of each bull market cycle. And our package of high-volatility no-loads provides *one huge middle*. Looks good on paper, but does it work?

Let's put it to the test.

Does It Work?

AFTER you've suffered through about twenty hours of eye strain, you'd be pretty upset if we'd come this far only to strike out. So it's time to see whether the wealth-building method we've developed has worked in the past. Keep in mind that there's absolutely *no guarantee* that the scheme will perform as well in the future as it has in recent years. But if our method has produced superior investment returns over long periods of time in almost every conceivable market environment, that should be a strong indication that we're on the right track. In this chapter, we'll give our whole wealth-building system a try. In fact, we'll try it out over one of the worst decades in stock market history—the period between the end of 1967 and the end of 1977.

On December 29, 1967, the Dow Jones Industrial Average closed at 905.11 on its way to another shot at the 1000 level. On December 30, 1977, that most conspicuous measure of stock prices stood at 831.17—about *8% lower* than it had been ten years earlier. You just don't see that kind of stagnation in

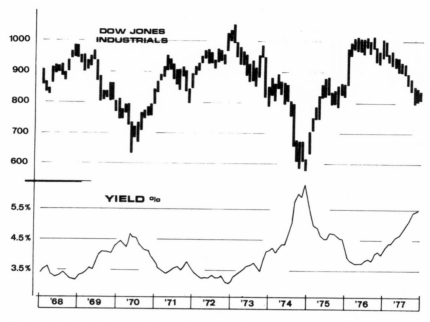

Chart 12-1. Dividend yield—Dow Jones Industrial Average, 1968–1977.

most ten-year periods. In terms of the odds, it's better than 3:1 that any single decade will be *better* than this one!

Chart 12-1 shows the whipsaw pattern of the Dow Jones Industrials over this rocky period: lots of roller coaster between the 600 level and the mystical 1000 barrier, but no real progress. I've also sketched in the dividend yield figures. They're calculated by dividing the monthly mean Dow Jones Industrial Index into the last four quarters' worth of dividends paid. You can get similar figures straight out of *Barron's*. As you can see, the dividend yield on the DJIA oscillated somewhat regularly, though far from uniformly, between the overvalued 3½% level and the undervalued 5½% level during the ten years. Based on the speculative cycles we've seen since stock trading began, this movement is fairly typical.

There are two key elements to our method. First, use only high-volatility no-load funds that tend to exaggerate the normal market cycle. And second, capture the expanded cycle by using a modified Variable Ratio plan based on undervalued/overvalued yield measures. Briefly but in detail, our techniques for buying into the package of no-load funds are:

1. Use your regular $100 payment to yourself each month to buy fund shares with yield ranges of 3¹/₂% to 4¹/₂%. These are moderate valuation levels where you can expect to receive the normal 10% to 12% return on your investments.

2. In addition to your $100 monthly investment, use *10% of your cash reserve* each month (10% monthly achieves roughly the same effect as 20% quarterly on a weighted average). With this cash, buy fund shares when the odds shift significantly toward you, becoming undervalued at 4¹/₂% to 5¹/₂%. You should expect investments made at these yields to return perhaps 15% or more on the basis of the long-term trends observed over the last forty years.

3. In addition to your $100 check, *use 20% of the remaining cash reserve* each month (adjusted from 50% quarterly) to buy fund shares when the market becomes an absolute bargain at yield levels in excess of 5¹/₂%. On those purchases you make when the market is grossly undervalued, you can expect to make 20% or more. Remember, buy more heavily as the odds get better.

As to selling: you're going to get defensive and *begin to withdraw 10% of your fund holdings* each month the market finds itself in overvalued territory—that's when dividend yields drop below 3¹/₂%. In the overvalued area, it's less than 50:50 that you'll make any money at all, so lighten up as the odds turn against you.

Again I'll emphasize two points. Under our plan, the speeds with which we get into and out of the funds are completely arbitrary. And our Variable Ratio plan will *never* catch the ultimate peak or the final trough precisely. That's not our purpose. Our objective is to *capture most of the bullish swing with most of our investment capital committed to the market*—that's why we need a magnified upside move. Then we hope to *withdraw most of our investment capital to the safety of a money-market (cash reserve) fund before it gets cremated in the bearish slide* that inevitably follows the speculative, overvalued binge. It's not realistic to expect precision from a plan that isn't designed for it! If it can hand you a respectable profit in a lousy market environment, especially when the experts are losing their shirts, that's all you can ask for. Over the long term, the plan should keep you moving in the right direction most of the time. When the opportunities are there for the taking, you'll have the cash to grab them. And when everyone else is playing the greater fool, you'll be heading for the exits. As long as cycles in stock prices persist, you'll be *betting with the odds,* not against them.

Finally, if, as we expect, our only really dynamic profits are going to come during the middle of the bull market phase, we're going to need some no-loads that will really scream. For the purposes of this test, we're going to use eight to ten no-loads that were actually *in existence during our Dreadful Decade,* and that were identified in the tout rags of the day as go-go funds. And we'll drop them only when they were dropped from the recommended lists of the advisory services.

For simplicity, I'm going to treat this group of funds as if it were one single fund. Its price index is compared to the New York Stock Exchange Composite Index in Chart 12-2 (both are referenced to 100 at the end of 1967). You can see that over this ten-year period the fund did swing up and down a lot faster than the NYSE Index but it didn't do much better, especially when the higher risk factor is considered. (All of which just reinforces my earlier thesis: it's virtually impossible to pick individual stocks that will significantly outperform the averages!) We picked our funds primarily on the basis of volatility, and it's obvious that, based on the percentages, this group of aggressive no-loads consistently outpaced the NYSE Index by a wide margin during bull markets. Just as consistently, it fell like a rock in bear markets. Overall, this group is about twice as volatile as the market averages. In other words, it gives us the big middle we need!

Fair enough test? I think you'll say yes. To get it started, we'll have to make some initial assumptions and address a few procedural details. Then we'll walk through the investment program you could have started ten years ago. We'll assume that you've done your homework: you've already developed your investment plan using a yield-directed Variable Ratio scheme. You've even managed to identify a few of the no-load go-go funds to use as your investment vehicle.

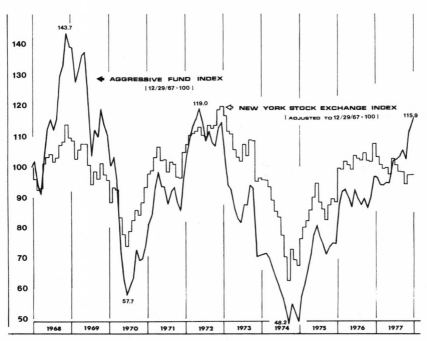

Chart 12-2. Aggressive fund index, January 1968 to December 1977.

We've already discussed the ante. Let's give you a thousand in cash to start with, and let's assume that you're willing to contribute faithfully a hundred every month to your plan. You don't have the foggiest notion that the ten years from 1968 to 1977 are going to be such a dismal departure from the prior ten, but you do have a generous portion of common sense; you're able to avoid pressure from the crowd and think for yourself. I'm going to assume that you'll make your investments at end-of-the-month prices. (In practice, there's a slight advantage to making your purchases on a Tuesday just before the last of the month and your sales on a Friday very early in the following month or around holidays. It's not enough of an edge to get excited about, but why not take every edge you can get?) Also I'll assume that you'll hold any cash reserve in a money-market fund that yields roughly a 6% annual rate paid monthly (that's close to the actual short-term rates that prevailed over this ten-year period, though rates went as high as 12% on occasion).

All right. Ready for a walk-through?

The tables grouped in Table 12-1 indicate month by month exactly what would have happened under our completed scheme. The whole thing looks pretty hairy, but it shows the operating details pretty clearly, so I'll try to explain it. The first numerical column gives the month-end *closing price* of the NYSE Index, with 12/29/67 equal to 100. The next column is the *average monthly yield* on the Dow Jones Industrial Average. We computed the yield gauge by averaging the DJIA's high and low closing prices during the month, and then dividing that result into the latest four-quarter total of dividends actually paid (if that sounds like too much work once you're on your own, essentially the same data can be found in the Market Laboratory section of *Barron's*). In column 3, we've listed a *fund price* index (again, 12/29/67 equal to 100) for our package of no-load funds, and that index is what we'll use to determine purchase price, redemption, and *market value of shares* held. Remember, there's no commission on a no-load, so what you give or get is the actual net asset value for each share. Column 4 lists the amount of money, determined solely by the DJIA yield criterion you're going to use for *stock purchases* in any month. It could be zero in an overvalued market, just your $100 monthly contribution in a normally valued market, or that $100 plus some percentage of your cash reserve in an undervalued market. Obviously, your *cash reserve* (column 9) will decline as you make larger purchases of fund shares, and will increase as you add your monthly contribution and the proceeds of *stock sales* (column 5) in an overvalued market. In the same way, of course, the number of *total shares held* (column 6) will decline when you sell fund shares, just as the cash balance will nearly always increase every month by the amount of *interest earned* (column 8) in addition to any other transfers into or out of cash. At the end of any month, after all the yield-dictated activities have been accomplished, you'll have some shares remaining in the fund that are priced at the fund index reading—this is the *market value* (column 7) of the shares you currently hold.

When you add the market value of your shares to your cash balance, you get the *total portfolio* shown in column 10: your net investment worth. Now that I've so lucidly explained the details, let's see if we can figure out what I said.

Flash back to Christmas of 1967. Other than the usual foul-ups that happen from time to time, it wasn't a bad Christmas. The Israelis and Egyptians had completed their regularly scheduled war that summer, the tragic exercise in Vietnam was visible and growing in its seriousness, but Johnson had promised us a "Great Society" and had repeatedly assured us that we could have both guns and butter. How much could have been haywire when the Beatles were stroking us with such classics as "Hey, Jude" and "Strawberry Fields Forever"? In short, not a shabby Christmas at all. Those were the days when an MBA had five job offers before his final exams were over, and his friend the engineering graduate had to fight off the head-hunters. Unemployment was running at its lowest level ever, and nobody seemed particularly worried about a 2% annual inflation rate. Compared to the Christmases that would follow, those were damn good days!

With only minor stumbles, the stock market had pressed relentlessly upward for nearly two decades, with prices expanding *tenfold* since the start of World War II. And nearly thirty million investors were convinced that "tenfold" was only the beginning. The economists were forecasting prosperity, the politicians promised abundance, and the masses became speculators. Everyone wanted a piece of the action. Your boss knew it, your neighbor knew it, and your old drinking buddy knew it. They'd just borrowed against their insurance policies to get more go-go. 1967 was a fabulous year . . . a boom year! And 1968 would be even better, it would be the best year of all. By late 1967, go-go fund performances were being measured in percentage gain per *month,* the leading conglomerate's earnings growth rates were accelerating, and it was obvious to everyone that there was no stopping the technology and efficiency of the great American industrial enterprise. What a rotten time to begin an investment program. An absolutely *terrible* time. Sooner or later, the frenzy had to run out of good news to feed on.

Table 12-1. Monthly transactions under the Variable Ratio plan (from 1968 to 1977).

	NYSE Index (12/29/67 =100)	Yield DJIA	Fund Price (12/29/67 =100)	To Purchase Stocks (4)	From Stock Sales (5)	Total Shares Held (6)	Market Value of Shares Held (7)	Interest Earned (8)	Total Cash Reserve (Initial $1,000)	Total Portfolio Value (10)	Gain or (Loss) (11)
1968											
Jan	96.0	3.42%	$102.0	—	—	—	—	—	$1,100	$1,100	—
Feb	92.5	3.56	93.8	$ 100	—	1.07	$ 100	$ 5	1,105	1,205	$ 5
Mar	93.0	3.62	91.0	100	—	2.16	197	6	1,111	1,308	8
Apr	101.2	3.38	102.9	—	$ 22	1.95	201	6	1,239	1,440	40
May	103.1	3.30	112.1	—	22	1.75	197	7	1,368	1,565	65
Jun	104.2	3.30	115.5	—	20	1.58	183	7	1,496	1,678	78
Jul	101.8	3.35	112.0	—	18	1.42	159	8	1,623	1,781	81
Aug	103.0	3.43	115.4	—	16	1.28	148	9	1,747	1,894	94
Sep	107.2	3.30	129.2	—	17	1.15	149	9	1,873	2,022	122
Oct	108.1	3.22	133.1	—	15	1.04	138	10	1,998	2,136	136
Nov	113.8	3.19	143.7	—	15	0.93	134	11	2,124	2,258	158
Dec	109.4	3.19	139.4	—	13	0.84	117	11	2,248	2,365	165
1969											
Jan	108.5	3.35	139.0	—	12	0.76	105	12	2,371	2,477	177
Feb	102.5	3.38	127.8	—	10	0.68	87	12	2,493	2,581	181
Mar	105.6	3.41	132.0	—	9	0.61	81	13	2,615	2,696	196
Apr	107.7	3.58	136.3	100	—	1.35	184	13	2,629	2,812	212
May	107.5	3.51	137.6	100	—	2.07	285	13	2,642	2,927	227
Jun	100.6	3.71	120.1	100	—	2.91	349	13	2,655	3,004	204

Jul	94.1	4.00%	$103.6	$ 100	—	3.87	$ 401	$13	$2,668	$3,069	$169
Aug	98.3	4.10	112.0	100	—	4.76	534	13	2,682	3,215	215
Sep	96.0	4.09	109.9	100	—	5.67	624	13	2,695	3,319	219
Oct	101.2	4.07	119.0	100	—	6.51	775	13	2,708	3,484	284
Nov	97.5	4.05	113.4	100	—	7.40	839	14	2,722	3,561	261
Dec	95.7	4.30	109.9	100	—	8.31	913	14	2,736	3,648	248
1970											
Jan	88.3	4.36	100.3	100	—	9.30	933	14	2,749	3,682	182
Feb	93.1	4.45	103.2	100	—	10.27	1,060	14	2,763	3,823	223
Mar	92.6	4.36	95.3	100	—	11.32	1,079	14	2,777	3,856	156
Apr	88.3	4.25	73.1	100	—	12.69	928	14	2,791	3,718	(82)
May	77.6	4.72	63.1	379	—	18.70	1,180	13	2,524	3,705	(195)
Jun	73.5	4.59	57.7	352	—	24.81	1,431	11	2,283	3,714	(286)
Jul	78.8	4.55	60.3	328	—	30.25	1,824	10	2,065	3,889	(211)
Aug	82.3	4.33	63.3	100	—	31.83	2,015	10	2,075	4,090	(110)
Sep	85.7	4.20	72.1	100	—	33.22	2,395	10	2,085	4,481	181
Oct	84.1	4.15	69.0	100	—	34.67	2,392	10	2,096	4,488	88
Nov	88.1	4.12	69.7	100	—	36.10	2,516	10	2,107	4,623	123
Dec	93.3	3.90	73.5	100	—	37.46	2,753	11	2,117	4,871	271
1971											
Jan	97.8	3.71	81.3	100	—	38.69	3,146	11	2,128	5,273	573
Feb	98.8	3.58	84.3	100	—	39.88	3,362	11	2,138	5,500	700
Mar	103.0	3.50	93.0	100	—	40.95	3,809	11	2,149	5,958	1,058
Apr	106.4	3.40	98.3	—	$403	36.86	3,623	13	2,665	6,288	1,288
May	102.0	3.42	93.5	—	345	33.17	3,102	16	3,125	6,227	1,127
Jun	102.3	3.51	93.3	100	—	34.24	3,195	16	3,141	6,336	1,136

Table 12-1 (continued). Monthly transactions under the Variable Ratio plan (from 1968 to 1977).

	NYSE Index (12/29/67 =100)	Yield DJIA	Fund Price (12/29/67 =100)	To Purchase Stocks (4)	From Stock Sales (5)	Total Shares Held (6)	Market Value of Shares Held (7)	Interest Earned (8)	Total Cash Reserve (Initial $1,000)	Total Portfolio Value (10)	Gain (Loss) (11)
Jul	98.1	3.58%	$ 87.9	$ 100	—	35.38	$3,110	$16	$3,156	$6,266	$ 966
Aug	101.7	3.61	91.9	100	—	36.47	3,352	16	3,172	6,524	1,124
Sep	100.9	3.51	93.2	100	—	37.54	3,499	16	3,188	6,687	1,187
Oct	96.7	3.60	88.4	100	—	38.67	3,419	16	3,204	6,623	1,023
Nov	96.3	3.81	85.5	100	—	39.84	3,407	16	3,220	6,627	927
Dec	104.8	3.59	96.1	100	—	40.88	3,929	16	3,236	7,165	1,365
1972											
Jan	107.2	3.42	103.7	—	$424	36.80	3,816	19	3,779	7,595	1,695
Feb	110.1	3.37	109.2	—	402	33.12	3,616	21	4,302	7,918	1,918
Mar	110.9	3.29	113.0	—	374	29.80	3,368	24	4,800	8,168	2,068
Apr	111.5	3.23	115.6	—	345	26.82	3,101	26	5,271	8,372	2,172
May	112.9	3.25	119.0	—	319	24.14	2,873	28	5,719	8,591	2,291
Jun	110.2	3.26	114.1	—	275	21.73	2,479	30	6,125	8,604	2,204
Jul	109.8	3.34	108.2	—	235	19.55	2,116	32	6,492	8,608	2,108
Aug	113.5	3.24	111.4	—	218	17.60	1,961	34	6,844	8,804	2,204
Sep	112.6	3.24	108.0	—	190	15.84	1,711	36	7,170	8,880	2,180
Oct	113.5	3.32	106.9	—	169	14.26	1,524	37	7,476	9,000	2,200
Nov	118.7	3.12	112.3	—	160	12.83	1,441	39	7,775	9,216	2,316
Dec	119.8	3.06	114.5	—	147	11.55	1,322	40	8,061	9,384	2,384

1973										
Jan	116.6	3.16%	$104.5	—	121	10.39	$1,086	$41	$8,324	$ 9,410	$2,310
Feb	111.5	3.32	94.0	—	98	9.35	879	43	8,564	9,443	2,243
Mar	110.7	3.39	92.6	—	87	8.42	779	44	8,795	9,574	2,274
Apr	105.4	3.46	86.6	—	73	7.58	656	45	9,012	9,668	2,268
May	103.0	3.55	83.1	$ 100	—	8.78	730	45	9,057	9,787	2,287
Jun	101.9	3.64	81.9	100	—	10.00	819	45	9,103	9,922	2,322
Jul	107.1	3.66	87.5	100	—	11.14	975	46	9,148	10,123	2,423
Aug	103.4	3.75	87.4	100	—	12.29	1,074	46	9,194	10,268	2,468
Sep	108.7	3.61	94.0	100	—	13.35	1,255	46	9,240	10,495	2,595
Oct	108.3	3.48	92.9	—	124	12.02	1,116	47	9,511	10,628	2,628
Nov	95.1	3.82	71.1	100	—	13.42	954	48	9,559	10,513	2,413
Dec	96.3	4.11	71.6	100	—	14.82	1,061	48	9,607	10,668	2,468
1974										
Jan	95.9	4.15	71.9	100	—	16.21	1,165	48	9,655	10,820	2,520
Feb	95.8	4.24	72.1	100	—	17.60	1,269	48	9,703	10,972	2,572
Mar	93.3	4.06	69.9	100	—	19.03	1,330	49	9,751	11,081	2,581
Apr	89.0	4.27	66.6	100	—	20.53	1,367	49	9,800	11,167	2,567
May	85.3	4.36	63.0	100	—	22.12	1,393	49	9,849	11,242	2,542
Jun	83.4	4.36	60.7	100	—	23.76	1,442	49	9,898	11,341	2,541
Jul	77.2	4.71	57.1	1,090	—	42.85	2,447	45	8,953	11,400	2,500
Aug	70.0	5.06	53.6	995	—	61.42	3,292	40	8,098	11,390	2,390
Sep	62.1	5.73	48.2	1,720	—	97.10	4,680	33	6,511	11,191	2,091
Oct	72.4	6.02	54.6	1,402	—	122.78	6,704	26	5,235	11,938	2,738
Nov	69.0	5.90	52.1	1,147	—	144.79	7,544	21	4,209	11,752	2,452
Dec	67.1	6.35	49.1	942	—	163.97	8,051	17	3,384	11,435	2,035

Table 12-1 (continued). Monthly transactions under the Variable Ratio plan (from 1968 to 1977).

	NYSE Index (12/29/67 =100)	Yield DJIA	Fund Price (12/29/67 =100)	To Purchase Stocks (4)	From Stock Sales (5)	Total Shares Held (6)	Market Value of Shares Held (7)	Interest Earned (8)	Total Cash Reserve (Initial $1,000)	Total Portfolio Value (10)	Gain or (Loss) (11)
1975											
Jan	76.0	5.64%	$ 56.8	$777	—	177.65	$10,090	$14	$2,721	$12,811	$ 3,311
Feb	80.0	5.18	61.0	372	—	183.75	11,209	12	2,461	13,669	4,069
Mar	82.1	4.93	65.6	346	—	189.02	12,400	11	2,226	14,626	4,926
Apr	85.8	4.93	70.4	323	—	193.60	13,630	10	2,013	15,643	5,843
May	90.0	4.61	77.3	301	—	197.50	15,267	9	1,821	17,088	7,188
Jun	94.5	4.54	80.8	282	—	200.99	16,240	8	1,647	17,887	7,887
Jul	88.3	4.53	76.7	265	—	204.44	15,681	7	1,490	17,171	7,071
Aug	86.0	4.75	74.0	249	—	207.81	15,378	7	1,347	16,725	6,525
Sep	82.6	4.73	71.1	235	—	211.11	15,010	6	1,219	16,229	5,929
Oct	87.4	4.67	73.6	222	—	214.13	15,760	5	1,102	16,862	6,462
Nov	89.6	4.54	74.6	210	—	216.94	16,184	5	997	17,181	6,681
Dec	88.5	4.56	74.3	200	—	219.63	16,319	4	902	17,221	6,621
1976											
Jan	99.5	4.09	87.1	100	—	220.78	19,230	4	906	20,136	9,436
Feb	99.1	3.85	91.9	100	—	221.87	20,390	5	911	21,301	10,501
Mar	101.8	3.78	92.6	100	—	222.95	20,645	5	916	21,561	10,661
Apr	100.5	3.73	89.8	100	—	224.06	20,121	5	920	21,041	10,041
May	99.0	3.74	86.8	100	—	225.21	19,549	5	925	20,473	9,373
Jun	103.5	3.75	92.7	100	—	226.29	20,977	5	929	21,907	10,707

Jul	102.7	3.83%	$ 89.6	$100	—	227.41	$20,376	$ 5	$ 934	$20,310	$ 9,010
Aug	102.0	3.89	87.4	100	—	228.55	19,975	5	939	20,914	9,514
Sep	104.5	3.82	89.8	100	—	229.67	20,624	5	943	21,567	10,067
Oct	102.0	4.07	86.2	100	—	230.83	19,897	5	948	20,845	9,245
Nov	101.8	4.12	89.9	100	—	231.94	20,851	5	953	21,804	10,104
Dec	107.5	3.99	96.9	100	—	232.97	22,575	5	958	23,532	11,732
1977										
Jan	103.1	4.29	96.5	100	—	234.01	22,582	5	962	23,544	11,644
Feb	100.7	4.34	94.2	100	—	235.07	22,143	5	967	23,111	11,111
Mar	99.4	4.46	94.0	100	—	236.13	22,196	5	972	23,168	11,068
Apr	99.7	4.60	94.8	197	—	238.21	22,583	4	879	23,462	11,262
May	97.6	4.74	94.7	188	—	240.20	22,747	4	795	23,542	11,242
Jun	102.4	4.59	102.0	180	—	241.96	24,680	4	719	25,399	12,999
Jul	100.5	5.01	102.3	172	—	243.64	24,924	3	651	25,575	13,075
Aug	98.3	5.25	103.2	165	—	245.24	25,308	3	588	25,897	13,297
Sep	98.1	5.37	105.6	159	—	246.74	26,056	3	532	26,588	13,888
Oct	94.1	5.49	102.3	153	—	248.24	25,395	2	481	25,876	13,076
Nov	97.3	5.40	111.7	148	—	249.57	27,864	2	435	28,299	15,399
Dec	97.5	5.62	115.9	187	—	251.14	29,107	2	350	29,457	16,457

You might have been a financial virgin in 1967, but right now, with the clock turned back, you're armed with a perspective on the speculative cycles gone by, and you have a guide that should force you in the right direction. With any luck at all, it'll keep you from losing your all when the promises of today turn into the broken hearts of the next cycle. And at Christmas of 1967, you never needed a guide more!

As you start your plunge into the world of high finance in January of 1968, the dividend yield guide on which you're basing your investment decisions sends out caution signals, so you hold back. Your first $100 monthly contribution goes directly into the money-market fund. Prices slip in February and March, and your initial purchases of $100 in each month buy 1.066 and 1.099 shares respectively at fund index prices, for total holdings of 2.165 shares after the third month. Current market value of the fund shares you hold is now $197.02 (2.165 × 91.0). Meanwhile, your end-of-January cash reserve ($1100) earns $5.50 interest in February and another $5.53 in March for a compound sum of $1111.03 at first quarter's end. Adding the market value of your fund shares held, $197.02, to the compound value of your cash reserve, $1111.03, puts the total value of your investment account at $1308.05. These are all the precise amounts. I figure you aren't too interested in the pennies, though, so our tables show everything except total shares rounded to the closest buck.

For the twelve months from April of 1968 through March of 1969, the market is operating in the overvalued area, with less than $3^{1}/_{2}$% current yield. According to your rules, it's time for you to do a little selling. In each of those twelve months, you'll sell off 10% of your existing fund shares at prevailing market prices, using the fund index for your sales, and you'll transfer the redemption proceeds into your money-market fund where it's safely earning interest. Notice that the shares-held balance declines every month as your progressive selling continues; your exposure to market risk is gradually being reduced. With only $200 worth of shares purchased in 1968, progressive selling out of an accumulated total of 2.16 shares may seem trivial, and I'll agree. This example is intended simply to illustrate the procedural details. Nevertheless, strict adherence to your plan should bring your market commitment down in a series of *very small* steps.

O.K. Let's move through the market's peak in December of 1968 and into what will eventually prove to be a severe bear market. You've got almost no exposure to loss at the top—only about 5% of your total wealth is in the market—and you don't begin taking on new fund shares until April of 1969. For the thirteen months between April of 1969 and April of 1970, the yield criteria indicate a fairly valued market (yield over $3\frac{1}{2}\%$, but less than $4\frac{1}{2}\%$) and you'll be increasing your commitment by purchasing only $100 worth of fund shares each month. Your progressive buying routine builds up a 25% invested position near the ultimate trough, contrasting with that 5% invested position near the previous peak. Notice, too, that while your cash position has grown by only the amount of interest earned for fifteen months, the increments were enough to build a large reserve that will let you make huge purchases in the next few months.

It's mid-spring of 1970 and here comes the bottom. You have absolutely no way of knowing that this will prove to be the final bottom, but the yield pointer is now sufficiently high (over $4\frac{1}{2}\%$) to indicate an undervalued situation. Not gross, but enough to tilt the odds more favorably toward you. So you'll bet more heavily on the improved odds. At April's end, you've got $2791 in your cash reserve. When yields rise above $4\frac{1}{2}\%$ in May, you'll use 10% of your reserve ($279), in addition to your normal $100 monthly contribution, to make a total purchase of 6.01 shares ($379/63.1) of the fund at depressed prices. A pair of transfers out of your money-market cash reserve into your aggressive no-load stock fund in June and July (each month in addition to the regular $100 input) buys 6.10 and 5.44 additional shares respectively and increases your market exposure to 47%. It's not the 100%-invested position you had hoped for at the final trough, but given the extremely high volatility of your fund, it's enough to realize sizable gains in the forthcoming bull market.

Let's back up for a second. Using monthly data, let's take a good look at your situation at the precise bottom of the market, which occurs at the June close. Virtually anyone who took the leap into the market when you did is sitting on a horrendous loss by that time—the NYSE Index is down more than 25% over the two and a half years, and your go-go has lost a staggering 40%. That's when it's really tough—for many people, next to impossible—to stick with simple-minded programs like Dollar Cost Averaging. To most people, it would take more guts than brains to throw another hundred bucks on top of a loss position that amounts to a thousand dollars or more. And that's why most investment plans fail. Now look at your profit or loss position at the ultimate low. True, it isn't a profit, but it isn't an incapacitating disaster either. You're down less than $300 on a total investment of $4000. You haven't won a pot yet, but you've still got most of your chips! And you're under no psychological pressure to quit just when it would be smarter to double your bet.

Life has many pleasures, and third or fourth on the list is the thrill of watching that screamer run up and seeing it fly! Once the raging bull takes over, you'll be checking the newspaper practically every day to see how you're doing. While most people will be waiting impatiently for a year or two just so they can get even and get *out,* you'll be ecstatic as that hummer takes off. So continue to average up, buying shares at higher and higher prices, even if you think the bottom has been passed. A word here on averaging up.

It's a lot smarter to average up than it is to average down. In fact, if you have to average down, buying on lower and lower prices, it's proof positive that most of your earlier decisions were wrong. You're not really thinking, you're operating on hope—hope that someday things will get better, that it will turn around and head up, and maybe even turn into a profit. On the other hand, when you're averaging up you know that your earlier actions were right, because you've already got a profit, and you have nothing to be concerned about except keeping the money you've made. Particularly when the market is in the early stages of recovery from a grossly undervalued condition, averaging up or even increasing your bet can be immensely profitable.

When all your contemporaries are using what they think is a bear market rally to cut their losses on the initial advance, bet your butt off. Let them be the bear market experts. The opportunity won't be there for long; a few months later when they've recognized the new bull market for what it really is, the dynamic gains will already have been posted. Pay absolutely no attention to those doomsayers who give you all the obvious reasons why the market must go down. They'll be the same prophets who knew all the obvious reasons why the market had to go up near its top two years ago. *Listen only to the market.* As long as every purchase you make increases your average cost, the market's letting you know you've been right. And when you're right in an undervalued area, there's a high degree of probability that you'll stay on the profit side for some time to come!

Let's press on. For another year and a half, except for two selling months in April and May of 1971, you'll continue to make your normal $100 purchases as your fund rises by two-thirds to the end of the year. Now it's early 1972. It's an election year, a mini-boom is in progress, and there's promise of peace in Vietnam. Suddenly everyone's hot on the stock market again. As usual, speculative enthusiasm drives market prices into the overvalued area, and the light flashes "caution." Sure, they still have a way to go to the final top, but the big gains are *behind* you, not ahead!

By January 1972 you're sitting on a pretty good-sized stack of chips, and it's probable that you've spent some time and energy honing your market timing skills. But let's say that you're still relying exclusively on the plan we've developed here. It's withdrawal time again. As prices surge to new peaks in early 1972, you continue selling shares to build cash. You're operating defensively, because you suspect that most of the upside progress in this cycle is already over. From a 55% market exposure in late 1971, you move to an invested position of less than 12% as the Dow Jones Industrials hit a new all-time peak in January of 1973. It's just after the Nixon landslide, and despite the market slide in the first few months of the new year, virtually everyone else is still sure the bull market will

continue. You, however, are in the process of building a 93%
cash reserve position. Smart work! The slide will get going in
earnest all too soon.

In seven out of the last eight months of 1973, you've been
nibbling at the market, but you've kept a padlock on the cash
box. You follow the same tactics for the first six months of
1974. You watched prices break 200 points in the six weeks
after the oil embargo was put into effect in the fall of 1973,
but, although you can't know it, you haven't seen anything yet.
The political instability, the uncertainty, the national psychosis
that manifests itself in the summer and fall of 1974 are radical
departures from the American post-war experience. Like the
attack on Pearl Harbor, the confusion that prevails in late
1974 creates once-in-a-generation deviations from intrinsic
values. Nobody, but nobody, could have forseen this tragic set
of events two years earlier; nobody could have predicted the
depths of national despair; nobody would have questioned, as
people now question, the very survival of our economic and
social system. You're scared (well, if you have any sense you're
scared), I'm scared, everyone is scared.

It sounds rotten to say it, but you're going to make a killing
out of this catastrophe. You're in a position to profit from it
because you've got two things that almost nobody else has . . .
guts and money. Without guts, you wouldn't act. Without
money, you couldn't act. But you've got both—your dividend yield plan is screaming, "This is it!" and you're holding
a cash box that's loaded with green. So you act. You use 10%
of your cash reserve in July and another 10% in August—over
37½ shares in just two months—as the market approaches its
final selloff. September, October, November, December . . .
gross undervaluations unlike anything since the late
1940s—20% of your remaining cash reserve each month into
your funds at the final lows—102½ shares in four fantastic
bargain months! In the last six months of 1974, you've raised
your exposure to 70% contrasted with only 7% at the market's
peak two years before. And you're holding a *net profit position,*
even though the Dow Jones Industrials have lost almost 500
points! With 70% of your money on the line in a package of

funds that has fallen two-thirds in six years, you discover the need for prayer.

The mood at Christmas of 1974 is entirely different from the mood of eight years earlier, when you began this wealth-building program. Then it looked as though stocks would never stop rising. Now it looks as though they'll never stop falling. In late 1967, the experts were predicting 1200 on the Dow within the year; now the same experts are saying 400. The only thing that's been going up lately is gold. And who would have thought that possible just a few years back? Gold has soared from $50 an ounce to $200 while the stock market has gone from 1000 to 600! And the experts are forecasting $300 for an ounce of gold within the year. No need to guess what happens. You already know.

The first half of 1975 turns out to be one of the best six-month periods in stock market history. The Dow Jones Industrials jump from under 600 into the mid-800s, the NYSE Index leaps ahead over 40%, and your fund soars almost 65%. Meanwhile, gold breaks sharply in a downtrend that will eventually halve its price. You felt pretty exposed last winter, but by summer your net investment worth totals half again as much as it did six months earlier. You've been averaging up on top of a profitable position. And you'll continue to use your dwindling cash reserve to average up through the correction that marks the last half of the pre-election year. By the end of 1975, you've got nearly 95% of your marbles on the line. Let's just hope that the tradition of election year bull markets will hold this time around.

The first month of 1976 is even better than January 1975, when the market burst out of the trough—the single-month gain of over 12% drives the market out of the undervalued territory. Happily, you've already used the bulk of your cash reserve when it counted most, and now your fund is even stronger, with a gain of over 17% to start the year. That, however, is just about it until after the election. (If you weren't in the market in January, then 1976 was pretty much of a waste.)

For the next year and three months, you continue to average up. By early 1977 it becomes apparent that your fund is tracing out a series of new highs. Meanwhile, the Dow Jones Industrial Average doesn't seem to be making any progress—in fact, it's dropping a bit, since the yield seems to be rising. That kind of split market, where most stocks rise while the Dow falls, is an extremely rare bird. It's caused by the efforts of the institutional money managers to create an indexed portfolio. This is a serious problem as we near the 1980s, so let's take a look at it. Since bank trusts, pension funds, insurance companies, and even some mutual funds haven't been able to beat the market averages over the years, they've decided that merely keeping up with the Standard & Poor 500 (a far better market reference, as it happens) is good enough for them. How's that for evidence that the professionals can't pick stocks any better than a dart can? Apparently the institutional managers held too many high-quality Dow-type stocks, and not enough issues of average quality and lower. So as they align their institutional portfolios to the S&P 500 Index, they have to sell off the overload of top-quality stocks, which creates a weakness in that group. They then snap up the secondary issues, and the rush generates strength in that sector. Since these institutions account for over two-thirds of the trading on the NYSE, the split is pretty wide. And no one can be sure just when the Dow Jones Averages will once again reflect what's actually happening in the market. It's been estimated that there are billions of dollars in the process of being indexed, and it's impossible to determine how long it will take to complete the process.

Back in early 1977, however, you and I aren't aware that our yield gauge, based on a distorted Dow Jones Average, is being bent out of whack. The Dow slides, the yield improves, and we're again getting undervalued readings, even though our fund has *nearly doubled* in just over two years. If the DJIA had kept pace with the average stock, it would stand at around 1200 instead of in the low 900s. But an undervalued reading dictates the use of 10% of your meager cash reserve, in addition to the normal $100 each month, to buy fund shares throughout the remainder of 1977. So you follow the rules.

Christmas 1977, ten years after you began the investment

process. Has it worked? Well, you're sitting on a stake of almost $29,500. It cost you $1000 to start with, $100 a month thereafter, some time and energy in the shuffle, and a little common sense. Has it worked? Hey, the Dow is *down* 8% in the last ten years and you've got a $29,500 stack of chips. You've turned around 16% per year on your invested capital, while the Dow has lost almost 1% a year. Think how big your take might have been if the Dow had gone up as it normally does. Is it fair to conclude that it works?

"Well, I'll agree that it might have worked in the past, but will it work in the future?" To that, my friend, I'll respond with an unqualified "I don't know." I think it will, but we're talking about an unknown. I can't guarantee what's going to happen tomorrow, or next week, or next month, or next year, any more than you can. I can only look at the past, pick a long enough slice of time to cover most of the high points and the lows, analyze it, and come up with something that worked in most markets then. To the extent that the future is similar to the long-term past, this set of guidelines should continue to work well. If Big Brother takes over, or if nations start slinging nuclear missiles at each other, or if the government continues to play insanity with the budget and the currency, who knows? Any investment program is predicated on the assumptions that the world isn't coming to an end, though it will probably seem to be on the brink from time to time, and that the ground rules of tomorrow will be about the same as the ground rules of today and yesterday.

Give me a little slack, admit that neither of us can do much to change the shape of the world, and let's make the flat assumption that the long-term future won't be too much different from the long-term past. Once we clear that hurdle, we can take a closer look at what we've got and see if there's anything we can do to make it work better.

First, what have we got? Our basic method is to use high-volatility no-load funds, and to change the percentage of our total assets committed to the market by a Variable Ratio model based on whether the market is undervalued or overvalued.

Now some qualifying points. First: our method is not designed to identify precisely the speculative top or the climactic trough of every cycle, or of any cycle, for that matter. We're averaging *into* the undervalued market in progressively larger amounts as it gets cheaper in relation to its normal value. And we're averaging out of the overvalued market. This weighted-averaging process makes our average cost based on the shares we purchase a lot *higher* than if we bought everything at the exact low, and it makes our average selling price *lower* than if we sold at the precise top. This means that our only chance for making a buck out of the cycle arises from holding larger investment positions during the *middle* of a bull market and, hopefully, larger cash positions during the *middle* of a bear market. Therefore, a big middle is crucial to making money with this scheme.

We spent a good deal of time back in the last chapter going over the selection process for the funds we wanted to use. Now you can see why we devoted so much paper to what might have seemed a rather trivial process. You've got to have a screamer to ensure the exaggerated cycle effect, so that that library assignment was very important. For our ten-year test, I used a package of eight to twelve funds that the tout rags of the day had already identified as the go-go no-loads. On the average, that sample moved up just over $2^{1}/_{2}$ times as fast as the market did, and fell about $1^{1}/_{2}$ times as fast. You'll need three or four no-loads with at least that much upside potential to implement a superior program. It'll take a couple of hours of research effort to cull the list and identify the movers, but it's time extremely well spent. You'll find several no-loads that consistently run up three or four times as fast as the market. So much the better!

The second point has to do with the precision, or lack of precision, of the Variable Ratio plan. I said as we were walking through the ten-year test that, after you've got a few thousand bucks on the line, you're probably going to get a lot more interested in improving the timing of your purchases and sales. After most ten-year periods following this scheme, you could reasonably expect to have an investment account amounting to twenty or thirty thousand bucks, maybe more. At some point, the $100 you plunk down every month just isn't as important as the active and intelligent management of the capital you've already accumulated. What happens to the $29,500 you're holding at the end of the ten-year test period is a lot more important to you than the number of new shares you're buying with your hundred-dollar contribution each month. In other words, the name of the game changes from wealth accumulation (getting it) to wealth management (keeping it and making it grow) after just a few years. *Since that's the case, you can forget about the $100 a month after a few years.* Spend it on a new set of wheels or threads or whatever—as long as you turn your energies toward improving the timing of your purchases and sales. How do you do that?

Read, study approaches, tinker, experiment on paper first, then play with a small portion of your actual cash. There are several lines of attack on the timing problem. Some work, most don't. But the odds that you'll be able to properly time the market's swings are a lot better than the odds that you'd be able to pick individual stocks that consistently outperform the market. So take heart, and keep testing. You've just spent twenty or thirty hours reading about a scheme for timing purchases and sales. There are about forty thousand derivative versions of this simple model we could have tried. For instance, how about *selling* at 15% a month, or 5%, or 20%, into an overvalued market? Or how about *buying* at 25%, 30%, or 50%, into an undervalued market? Or how about redefining our undervalued/overvalued criteria—why not 5.25% and 3.25%? There are literally thousands of options. We could get a computer, collect all the data, whip out some fancy optimization techniques, and fire away at the countless versions, and maybe we'd find greater precision. Maybe you don't have to go that far, but as I said, once your money's on the line, you'll get turned on to making it work hard on your behalf.

One final point has to do with the yield measure we've used to guide our investment actions. There's the question of just what level of yield constitutes a fairly valued, overvalued, undervalued, or grossly undervalued market: why not eight or ten classifications with different buy/sell rules for each? But there's the more serious problem of the current distortion in the Dow Jones Industrial Average on which we're basing our decisions.

As I indicated a few pages back, the Dow's suffering from the latest fad of indexing institutional portfolios—putting extraordinary pressure on the highest-grade stocks and propping up some of the lower grades. Unfortunately, there's no telling how long that aberration is going to last. For eighty years, the Dow Jones Industrial Average has been "the market" to most investors, but the fact is that it no longer represents the true price trends or valuation levels of the overwhelming majority of stocks. In other words, somebody bent our ruler! And the logical solution—to get a new measuring tool—requires a little effort. "What, again?!" Yes, but this time, not much.

Essentially the same criteria for undervaluation and overvaluation as we've used here can be applied to a better but less widely publicized market reference, one we've already met: Standard & Poor's Composite Index. And we'll get similar results. Most big-city newspapers carry the S&P 500 data—check the Sunday financial section particularly—and you can also find them in *Standard & Poor's Outlook,* a publication that's available in most libraries. Where you can find the S&P yield data, I'd recommend that you use it instead of the Dow Jones Industrial figures.

Enough of the details. We've applied some common sense to the problem, we've determined the odds, we've chosen the vehicle, we've bet *with* the odds, and we've built a good-sized stack of chips. You've still got some homework to do. I'm going to get a glass of wine.

Wrap-Up

WE'VE just spent two hundred or so pages together discussing how to get money, how to keep it, and how to make it grow. And we've covered a lot of principles. If we've arrived at any single conclusion, it's that you can get rich—or at least come awfully close—*if* you'll think about it, plan for it, and carry out your plan. Most people will never even give it a try because they're firmly convinced that they're trapped by circumstances. But you and I now know that there's a way out of the working-for-the-man syndrome.

Without any question, the basic requirement for achieving the security and independence money can help to provide is a *plan*, a reasonable plan for taking a few bucks a day and running it into a stake of twenty or thirty thousand dollars within ten years or so. The first twenty or thirty are the hardest. After that, time and compounding will take care of the rest.

We began with an overview of the planning process . . . examining your current financial condition, deciding where you want to be financially in the future, and asking how you're

going to get from here to there. All of this led to just one critical decision: your decision to *pay yourself first*.

Then we went further into the details of the wealth plan:
the importance of high earnings rates, the risks you'd have to
accept to get them, the necessity for diversification, the impact
of taxes, and the investment media options available to you.
All this led to the conclusion that the stock market is where
you have to start the wealth-building process.

Finally we developed a specific strategy designed to take
advantage of the speculative cycles that recur in the stock market. We constructed the approach by taking bits and pieces
from the simple formula plans, by learning the betting odds in
the stock market, and by measuring the market's undervalued
or overvalued condition. To see if it was any good, we put the
whole wealth-building system to the test.

And it worked—to the tune of almost $30,000 ac-
cumulated over one of the worst ten-year periods in the stock
market since the Depression era. I'm giving you no guarantees
that it'll work as well in the 1980s or the 1990s. But it worked
in the 1940s, the 1950s, the 1960s, and the early 1970s—and
that's a reasonable indication that you can expect to turn $3 a
day into $20,000 or $30,000 in most 10-year periods. And
that's the stake you need to get started. In the process of accumulating the first twenty or thirty thousand, you'll also develop a considerable degree of expertise. You'll gain the capability and the confidence to manage your own money better
than anyone else could for you.

Before we close off, let me tell you why I wrote this book
in the first place. There's one important reason you couldn't
know, though I think I hinted at it earlier. You deserve a better start than I got. I don't pretend to know all the things you
should do to make a million in the stock market, but I sure do
know a few things you *shouldn't* do. So let me spend the last
few pages telling you how I got started in this investment process. You see if you can spot my mistakes.

I'd worked for a while in the 1960s and had managed to
save a few bucks which I had, following tradition, stashed in
the bank. One night, a few of the guys I hung around with
were telling war stories about their successes in the stock

market—an interesting change of topical pace in those days. The prospect of money without effort! I was fascinated. Sometimes I'm baffled by my own gullibility, but I honestly believed those tales of conquest. All you had to do was to buy a "good" stock in a "growth" industry and let it run. Within a few days, I was chasing down every "make a million" book I could get my fat little fingers on, and within a few weeks I was learning how to adjust balance sheet inventory valuations for differences in accounting methods. These refinements, of course, along with a few even more esoteric procedures, were supposed to lead to more accurate estimates of corporate earnings. Then, after I had assigned an "appropriate" multiplier to the estimated earnings, I would assuredly know what the stock was *really worth*. From there on, it was going to be easy. If the stock was selling in the market for less than its true worth, it was a buy; for more than its true worth; it was a sell. That's what the prevailing wisdom said: scrutinize the financial statements, project earnings, throw in a little something for quality of management, assign a price/earnings ratio—and *boom*, there it was, the road to riches.

I liked airplanes in those days, as well as electronics. Both were hot! We had already got involved in southeast Asia, so it was obvious to me that we'd need airplanes to drop the bombs. And our airplanes would need radars to shoot down the enemy airplanes (who knew that the entire North Vietnamese airforce at the time consisted of seven Piper Cubs?). I had found a couple of industry groups that *had* to grow like wildfire. After confirming my own hopes with the latest brokerage firm research reports on both groups, I was ready to play big shooter.

I was living in Los Angeles at the time, and my stockbroker was a freshly minted MBA out of one of the prestige schools. He had been recommended by a friend as a real gunslinger who always seemed to pick the hot ones. A few hours of discussion and we found *the one*—a leading aerospace company with a strong electronics subsidiary. O.K., we were ready to go! The date was February 9, 1966—the Dow Jones Industrials were crossing the magic 1000 mark for the first time in history. (There were cheers, actual cheers, in the boardroom

on this auspicious occasion.) At that exact instant, I was pl~ ~~
ing down just over four thousand dollars for one hundred
shares of Airelec, which was highly recommended for aggressive accounts by the brokerage firm's research analyst and our
choice for my fortunes. I was just like a kid with a new toy. No
more staid old savings account for me, I had got in on the action. All that cheering, I figured, must be because I'd joined
the club.

Did I ever join the club! I'd committed about five of the
worst mortal sins by jumping in at that particular time—I'd
bought *one stock* in a *hot group* in an *overspeculated market* with
all my money because it seemed the way to *get rich quick!* "Not to
worry," said the kid with the MBA, "we're gonna make a bundle on this!" With those pearls of wisdom compounding my
confidence, I trundled off toward the door. As I glanced back
over my shoulder on the way out, the electronic display board
read: Dow Jones Industrial Average—998.73. A pullback . . .
maybe I should leverage it to the hilt and buy some more?

I wasn't a worrier back then. Had a job, chased around,
generally raised as much hell as I could. And the last thing I
worried about was my stock. The broker had said not to worry
and I didn't. Dumb, because I not only didn't worry, I *didn't
even watch!* Not, at least, until late summer. Must have been
August or September. I was having breakfast with a buddy
one morning after class. I was sitting there reading the sports
section of the Los Angeles *Times* when he asked me how to
read the financial pages. Since the financial section is right in
back of the sports section in the *Times,* it seemed easy enough
to explain the intricacies of the stock market using my
hundred shares of Airelec as an example. So I turned the
page and there it was:

high	low	name	div	sales	open	high	low	close	chg
.	.	.	.	.	.	.	.	.	.
.	.	.	.	.	.	.	.	.	.
42¼	21½	Airelec Corp	1.10	306	22½	23¼	22¼	22¼	−½
.	.	.	.	.	.	.	.	.	.
.	.	.	.	.	.	.	.	.	.

My God, 22¼! What happened to my four thousand
bucks? I've lost almost $1800 in less than nine months! That

can't be! We figured that Airelec was a $60 or $70 stock on this year's earnings alone . . . not even counting new military contracts that were sure to boost next year's earnings. Panic! No, panic and rage. Mostly panic, but I was set to kill the son-of-a-gunslinger who'd got me into this mess! (Notice that I've shoved the responsibility for this loser off onto someone else's shoulders? Naturally, I would have taken full credit for being a financial genius if it had gone up instead.)

I broke every traffic law in the Los Angeles municipal code on my way down to the brokerage house. And I was more than exasperated when the receptionist announced that the kid had moved to another firm way off in Atlanta. However, Mr. Righttrack might be willing to accept me as a client. Righttrack was in complete contrast to the gunslinger. He was more restrained in his enthusiasm. He was older and wiser, kind of like Solomon in a vested grey pinstripe. Righttrack had lived through quite a few bear markets, and he knew that recession-proof industries were the only way to survive when the economy was faltering. By September and October of 1966, the telltale signs of an impending business contraction were beginning to show.

Old Righttrack seemed to know what he was doing so, after a couple of weeks of deliberation, we decided to get out of that speculative aerospace/electronics stock into something that was sure to survive next year's recession. Sounded reasonable. The market was headed straight south anyway (the Dow Jones Industrials were in the mid-700s by this time), so it seemed prudent to get into a defensive grocery chain stock before we got cremated. All right, we'll swap Airelec for Safestore and cover ourselves against "serious price erosion."

If I made a few mistakes when I joined the club in February, I had just compounded them ten times over by switching from an aggressive position to a defensive position in October of 1966. I'm still playing *one* stock, but now I'm running *scared* in a *panicked market* with *all my money* and my motive is *fear*. What has happened is that I've lost all sense of perspective, and it's the reason I'm losing so regularly. I let the cover of *Newsweek* tell me that I've lost my shirt, just as it'll tell me two years from now that . . . well, we already know what came up next. Only one of the greatest bull market periods for marginal stocks in history—some doubled, redoubled, and doubled again. Safestore? From the low-20s to the mid-20s. As Righttrack said later, "Well, you just don't expect defensive stocks to move up too fast in a bull market. After all, they're supposed to be stable."

Now, my whole purpose in telling you how I got into investing is not to prove beyond the shadow of any reasonable doubt that I'm entirely inept, but so that you can learn a lesson from my errors. Since I've made at least my fair share of poor investment decisions, there are quite a few things that I know *don't work*. Incidentally, these aren't my mistakes alone. Ask any one of the seven or eight million people who've quit the stock market game in the last ten years. Losers can't afford to play very long! To keep you from joining them, I'll try to capsulize the important mistakes that can ruin your financial future.

Mortal Sins

1. *Don't invest.* Blow it away! Better yet, don't worry about wasting your money. Give up any and all aspirations you may have had for financial security and independence. After all, what with welfare, bankruptcy court, and Social Security, the "system" will take care of all your needs.

2. *Save, but keep all your money in a safe place.* Put it in the bank or in an insurance policy where it compounds at a miser's rate, where inflation gnaws away at its purchasing power, and where the government taxes you on every last nickel of earnings—a slow, steady, and guaranteed way to lose!

3. *Always rely on the opinions of the experts.* Always believe that the government is telling you the truth, that your employer has your best interests at heart, and that the tooth fairy will leave you a dime—based on past performance.

4. *Always stay fully committed to the market.* Stocks will keep going up forever, real estate prices will keep increasing stead-

ily each year, gold is a cinch to double in the next two years—spring is the only season.

5. *Pick one stock that will outperform the market.* Analyze the 2200 stocks on the NYSE, the 1200 on the AMEX, and the 2500 actively traded OTC with your hand calculator, and pick the one with outstanding potential. You'll be the first to discover the secret!

6. *Buck the odds.* Buy stocks when you've got some extra money from working overtime and when business conditions look strong. Then sell them if the economy doesn't look good or if you really nead the money because of a layoff. Join the crowd—you'll be close to 100% dead wrong.

There are hundreds of venial investment sins we could list, but these are the real biggies. These are the ones that could kill you! Just because you don't commit them doesn't guarantee your financial success, but it's absolutely impossible to make these mistakes for very long—simply because you'd lose it all!

I don't want us to wind up our discussion on a sour note, since what I'm trying to say is just the opposite. Money is a very positive subject; after all, it goes a long way toward providing the security and independence both of us want and need. A lot of people have said, rightfully, that money can't buy happiness. What they imply, whether they intend to or not, is that having money and being happy are mutually exclusive goals. Ridiculous. It's not an either/or choice, and there's no reason you can't have both.

The plans and strategies we've explored here ought to be a very strong indication that you and I can both make it on our own. Frankly, a good, well-thought-out financial plan and a workable strategy for arriving at our wealth objectives are about 90% of the battle. Once we've got those, the specific tactics follow pretty logically. We've examined the odds and we know them fairly well by now. Over the years, as long as we continue to *place our bets with the odds in an essentially favorable game,* there's every reason to expect that we'll have a huge stack of chips well before the last hand is played.

Index